Crafting Clean

The Art and Science of Handmade Soap

Hannah Thompson

Table of Contents

INTRODUCTION

The fascinating world of handmade soap-making is explored in depth in "Crafting Clean: The Art and Science of Handmade Soap." The book, written by a professional soap craft enthusiast, skillfully combines the precise science of creating handcrafted soaps with the artistic appeal of handicrafts. Through painstaking attention to detail and comprehensive directions, the author shares the secrets of creating original soap formulas that make use of a variety of scents, colors, and textures. The book supports both novice and seasoned soap makers, including everything from basic ingredients to sophisticated procedures, and cultivates a community of enthusiastic crafters.

"Crafting Clean" goes beyond superficial beauty to explore the complex science behind soap chemistry while making sure that readers understand the vital balance of ingredients, lye, and oils. With step-by-step instructions accompanied by vivid illustrations, the book transforms the seemingly complex process into an accessible and enjoyable craft. Additionally, it supports ethical ingredient procurement and sustainable processes, supporting the growing need for environmentally friendly substitutes. Aspiring soap artists will discover that the endless possibilities for creativity are inspiring as well as empowering, providing them with the expertise to make soap that is not only aesthetically pleasing but also mild and nourishing for the skin. "Crafting Clean" is an all-inclusive manual that celebrates the union of art and science in making beautiful handcrafted soaps

CHAPTER I

The Basics of Soap Making

Understanding The Ingredients

The art of crafting handmade soap is a delicate dance of chemistry and creativity, with a deep understanding of the ingredients playing a pivotal role in the process. Fats and oils are at the heart of any handmade soap recipe, chosen for their unique properties and contributions to the final product. These can range from vegetable oils like olive, coconut, and palm to animal fats such as tallow or lard. Each type of fat or oil brings distinct qualities to the soap, influencing factors such as hardness, lather, and moisturizing capabilities. Achieving the right combination of these ingredients is essential for creating a soap that cleanses and provides a luxurious and nourishing experience for the skin.

One of the critical ingredients in soap making is lye, also known as sodium hydroxide. Lye is a powerful alkali that initiates saponification, transforming fats and oils into soap. While lye is necessary, it requires careful handling and precise measurement. Too much lye can result in a harsh and potentially irritating soap, while too little may lead to a product that fails to cleanse effectively. Soap producers must maintain a careful balance to ensure that all of the lye is used up throughout the saponification process and that there is no leftover lye in the finished soap.

Understanding the properties of different fats, oils, and lye empowers soap makers to tailor their creations to specific preferences and skin types. For example, coconut oil contributes to a bubbly lather, making it a popular choice for those who enjoy a foamier cleansing experience. Olive oil, on the other hand, brings moisturizing qualities, making it suitable for individuals with dry or sensitive skin. The versatility of handmade soap lies in the ability to customize these ingredients, catering to a diverse range of needs and preferences.

Beyond the fundamental components, handmade soap offers an array of additional ingredients that contribute to the overall character of the product. Essential oils from plants impart fragrance to the soap, allowing soap makers to create a sensory experience beyond mere cleansing. Natural colorants, herbs, and botanicals can be used to improve the visual appeal and add texture to the soap. These extra ingredients enhance the soap's visual appeal and may have medicinal advantages depending on the essential oils and botanicals selected.

Ethical considerations and a desire for sustainability often influence the choice of ingredients in handmade soap. Many artisans opt for plant-based oils and jars of butter, catering to consumers seeking cruelty-free and environmentally friendly options. Thanks to the handmade soap-making process' transparency, consumers may make well-informed decisions and match their values with the products they use. The recent interest in handmade soaps can be attributed to this emphasis on natural and ethical components.

Furthermore, handmade soap makers often continuously learn and experiment to refine their craft. The world of soap-making is dynamic, with new ingredients and techniques constantly emerging. This commitment to innovation ensures that the art of handmade soap remains vibrant and responsive to evolving consumer preferences.

In conclusion, understanding the ingredients of handmade soap is fundamental to soap making. The careful selection and combination of fats, oils, lye, and additional elements allow artisans to create unique and personalized products. This craft goes beyond mere cleansing, offering a sensory and indulgent experience that reflects a commitment to quality, ethics, and sustainability. This old but ever-evolving craft continues to evolve, and the growing desire for natural and artisanal products underscores the importance of knowing what ingredients are in handcrafted soap.

Essential Tools and Equipment

Starting a handmade soap-making adventure necessitates a thorough comprehension of the fundamental tools and supplies that are the foundation of any artistic undertaking. Various multipurpose instruments that enable accurate measuring, thorough mixing, and careful shaping are essential to soap-making. Among these, a dependable scale is essential for allowing soap producers to measure the oils and lye precisely, which is necessary for a good batch. Accuracy is essential because minute variations can affect the chemical equilibrium required for saponification. A wide range of heat-resistant receptacles for mixing and reheating components are equally necessary. Heat-resistant plastic or stainless steel is ideal for the oils and lye solution to mix well without losing their integrity.

Precise thermometers go hand in hand with scales and containers. Controlling the temperature is essential to the soap-making process since it affects both the quality of the finished product overall and the effectiveness of saponification. When lye and oils are mixed, temperature should be monitored to ensure the chemical reaction proceeds as best, producing safe and effective soap. Also, a high-quality thermometer helps to enhance the sensual and visual attractiveness of the soap by helping to determine when to add fragrance oils, colorants, or other ingredients.

An immersion blender is a game-changer in soap production. Blending oils and lye efficiently takes skill to get the desired trace or the point at which the soap batter thickens. The immersion blender streamlines this process, ensuring a smooth and consistent texture while requiring less time and effort. Its adaptability allows for creating complex swirls and designs inside the soap, enhancing the craft's creative quality.

There are many different sizes and forms of molds that soap manufacturers use as their canvas. The ultimate shape of the soap is determined by the mold used, which ranges from traditional rectangular molds to complex silicone molds that produce distinctive designs. Artisans can showcase their ingenuity through the visual appeal of handmade soap using silicone molds with elaborate designs or wooden molds lined with parchment paper, catering to various preferences. In keeping with the increasing desire for eco-friendly methods, a dedication to sustainability may prompt soap producers to investigate reusable molds or ones made of eco-friendly materials.

Protective gear forms a vital part of the soap maker's toolset to guarantee safety and accuracy. Gloves screen the hands from direct contact with acidic substances, and goggles cover the eyes from any droplets of lye solution. It is essential to have a well-ventilated workspace with a dependable exhaust fan or adequate ventilation to dissipate any fumes produced during the soap-making process. Setting safety precautions as a top priority aid in a seamless and pleasurable crafting experience while protecting the artist.

The last touch to the soap-making process is a curing rack, which gives the freshly molded soap a specific place to go through this stage. This step is essential for the soap to solidify, allowing the water to evaporate and the saponification process to finish. There must be sufficient air movement around the curing soap to dry evenly and thoroughly. Racks made of wood or stainless steel with plenty of space between the bars help to keep the soap from adhering and encourage adequate curing.

Besides the material instruments, knowledge is a vital resource for a soap producer. Having access to credible books, websites, or discussion boards promotes lifelong learning and skill development. Knowing the properties of various oils, the nuances of mixing fragrances, and the science underlying saponification allows soap makers to explore and develop their craft. Getting involved in an artist community offers a forum for exchanging insights, resolving problems, and getting ideas from various viewpoints.

Some craftsmen may use digital tools in their soap-making process as technology develops. Like this one, recipe calculators help determine the exact number of oils and lye needed for a given batch size, which expedites the planning stage. Social media and online platforms are great places to share and exhibit works, meet like-minded people, and learn about the newest methods and trends in the soap-making world.

The essentials for making handmade soap are the cornerstone of the craft's science and creativity bloom. Every tool, from precise measuring instruments to safety equipment and creative molds, uniquely influences the soap maker's experience. The fusion of traditional equipment and contemporary aids and a dedication to safety and education guarantees a gratifying and rewarding experience for artists engaged in this age-old skill as they create distinctive, premium, handcrafted soaps.

Safety Precautions

Making soap by hand is a fun and fulfilling project that enables artisans to produce one-of-a-kind, customized goods. However, safety must come first to guarantee a safe and happy crafting experience, even amid the artistic thrill of creating soap. One of the most important things to consider is how lye, a potent alkali used in the saponification process, is handled. Sodium hydroxide, or lye, is an acidic substance that must be used carefully. When handling lye, always wear the proper protective gear, such as gloves and goggles. Unintentional spills and splashes can seriously irritate eyes and skin. Furthermore, pick an area with enough ventilation, or think about utilizing an exhaust fan to assist spread out any contaminants that might come up during mixing.

Pay close attention to the suggested safety precautions when mixing lye with water. Water should always be added to lye, not the other way around, to avoid splattering and strong reactions. To reduce fume exposure, stir the mixture carefully and stay a safe distance away. A distraction-free workspace and plenty of uninterrupted time to concentrate on soap-making are essential. To reduce the chance of unintentionally coming into contact with lye or other potentially dangerous materials, it is best to have a specific area set aside for making soap, away from kids and dogs.

The protective gear range includes closed-toe shoes, long sleeves, gloves, and goggles. The possibility of unintentional skin contact with lye solution is reduced when suitable clothing is used. Establishing a defined place for first aid is essential in case of accidental exposure. Have vinegar available to counteract lye on the skin, and ensure you have water access to flush the afflicted areas. Know where the emergency exits are located, and make sure you have a plan for dealing with unforeseen circumstances.

Also, controlling temperature is essential for producing soap. The lye solution and the oils must be at the proper temperature range for saponification to be effective. Maintain temperature awareness and prevent overheating by using trustworthy thermometers. The saponification process can accelerate quickly at high temperatures, which causes the soap batter to thicken before it can be put into molds. The final soap's texture and appearance may suffer as a result. As you add scents, colorants, or additives, please pay attention to the temperature because some may require a specific temperature to be well incorporated.

Careful handling is necessary when using specialized instruments in the soap-making process, in addition to worries about temperature. Splatters can result when using immersion blenders, frequently used to combine oils and lye. To avoid accidental splashing, ensure the blender is completely submerged in the soap batter before starting. To prevent air bubbles from forming during mixing, which could affect the texture of the soap, move the blender carefully. To keep control over the process, think about blending slowly and steadily. Additionally, secure storage and labeling of ingredients are crucial safety precautions when manufacturing soap.

All containers should be clearly labeled to prevent confusion and possible mix-ups. Keep ingredients out of children's reach and store them somewhere cold and dry without sun exposure. Take care when working with essential oils as well, as some might irritate skin or trigger allergic reactions. Learn about the characteristics of each essential oil and use the right safety measures, such as wearing gloves, when handling them.

Ensure the molds and equipment are clean and in good working order before using them. Mold contamination can lower the soap's quality, and broken equipment could be dangerous. Check for wear or malfunction on tools like immersion blenders regularly. Develop a rigorous mold cleaning regimen to avoid cross-contamination between batches. A safe and effective soap-making process is facilitated by equipment upkeep.

Handmade soap should be stored and cured carefully to avoid damage and to prolong its shelf life. Handling cured soap with gloves is best because it might be harsh. To ensure the soap has solidified and is safe, give it enough time to heal completely before using it. Sufficient curing time prolongs the life of the soap by averting premature degradation and softness.

Another aspect of safety when making soap is considering the environment. Maintaining sustainable habits benefits the environment and human health. Some of these practices include choosing ethically sourced materials and using eco-friendly packaging. With the increasing demand for eco-friendly products, soap makers are better equipped to meet ethical standards and improve the overall safety of their craft by including environmentally sensitive alternatives.

Finally, it should be noted that when making handcrafted soap, safety measures must come first. For a safe and joyful soap-making experience, every step—from handling caustic materials like lye to temperature control, appropriate labeling, and equipment maintenance—must be well thought out. Craftspeople may confidently produce beautiful handmade soaps by incorporating safety measures into every process step. This way, they know they have done all essential safety measures to safeguard themselves, their surroundings, and anybody who could come into touch with the finished product.

CHAPTER II

The Science Behind Soap

Chemical Processes Involved in Soap Making

The fascinating art of creating soap calls for several complex chemical reactions that turn raw materials into a nourishing and cleaning finished good. The basic process known as saponification lies at the center of this alchemical transformation. When fats or oils, generally in the form of triglycerides, combine with an alkaline material —usually potassium hydroxide for liquid soap or sodium hydroxide (lye) for solid soap—a chemical reaction occurs. These fats end up being converted into glycerine and soap. This reaction is essential to soap production since it determines the quality, texture, and washing capabilities of the end product.

Appropriate oil and lye measurements are necessary to start the saponification process. The glycerol backbone of three fatty acid chains is what makes up the triglyceride molecules present in oils. Lye, a potent alkaline solution, hydrolyses these triglycerides into fatty acids and glycerol. Triglycerides break down because of the interaction between the hydroxide ions from the lye and their ester linkages. Glycerol and free fatty acids are produced due to this separation, which prepares the way for the following stages of the saponification process.

After the fatty acids and glycerol are freed, they proceed through esterification. The soap molecules, which are sodium or potassium salts of the fatty acids, are created during the esterification process when the fatty acids mix with the hydroxide ions in the lye. As a result of this reaction, fatty acids are changed into carboxylate ions, which create a new molecule. Water and soap molecules are created when these carboxylate ions combine with the sodium or potassium ions from the lye. Because the soap molecules have both hydrophobic (which repels water) and hydrophilic (which attracts water) components, they are amphiphilic. Soap molecules interact with water and oil due to their amphiphilic nature, making removing grime and grease from surfaces easier.

As a natural byproduct, the glycerol generated during saponification is retained in the soap. Glycerine, sometimes called glycerol, is a vital ingredient with moisturizing qualities. Handmade soaps are both purifying and nourishing for the skin since they draw and hold water, which helps to maintain skin hydration. Glycerine is one of the key ingredients that distinguishes homemade soap from soap that is produced commercially. This is because many commercial methods remove glycerine so that it may be used in other goods, which may leave the soap less moisturizing.

One of the most essential factors in deciding the final soap product is the temperature at which the saponification occurs. Temperature control guarantees that the reaction progresses as best, enabling complete mixing and averting unfavorable problems. The exothermic character of saponification refers to the heat-producing response that occurs when oils and lye are combined. This temperature increase helps keep the soap batter fluid, making adding colorants, perfumes, or other ingredients more accessible. On the one hand, too much heat can cause saponification to speed up, thickening the soap batter more quickly and possibly changing the final texture and look of the soap.

Trace is the stage that the soap mixture reaches after the saponification process is finished. When the soap batter comes trace, the soap maker can safely pour the mixture into molds because it has thickened enough. The achievement of trace indicates the successful saponification reaction and the soap's stable state for subsequent processing. The kind of oils used, the temperature, and the mixing technique are some of the variables that can affect how long it takes to reach trace.

After being poured into molds, soap undergoes a curing period. During this crucial phase, the soap becomes harder and loses moisture. This stage ensures a solid and durable soap by allowing extra water from the saponification process to evaporate. Depending on the particular soap formulation and desired qualities, a period ranging from weeks to months may pass during the curing process. The texture, lathering capabilities, and shelf life of cured soap all improve.

Recognizing the function of additives in the soap's formulation is essential to comprehending the chemistry of soap-making. Certain fragrances add to the soap's sensory appeal. These aromatic molecules, which can be produced from fragrance or essential oils, are added at precise stages of the soap-making process to maintain their subtle fragrances. While fragrance oils give a wider variety of aromas, essential oils, produced from plants, offer natural and therapeutic fragrance possibilities.

Colorants are an additional type of additive that improves the aesthetic appeal of handcrafted soap. Manufacturers of soap are able to create a visually appealing color palette by utilizing a variety of natural and synthetic ingredients, including as micas, clays, and powdered botanicals. The result of the soap is influenced by the colorants chosen and mixed into the soap batter, which promotes artistic expression in the craft.

Adding botanicals, herbs, and exfoliants to soap compositions adds a new level of complexity to the chemical makeup. The skin advantages of oatmeal, lavender buds, or calendula flowers extend beyond their aesthetic value. These organic components give the finished soap product texture, color, and therapeutic benefits.

The chemical reactions that create soap demonstrate how simple elements may be transformed into valuable and adaptable finished goods. Triglyceride hydrolysis, fatty acid esterification, the synthesis of soap molecules, and the production of glycerol are all part of saponification, the primary reaction at the core of the soap-making process. A premium handcrafted soap results from meticulous temperature control, trace achievement, and the following curing process. Knowing the chemistry in creating soap enables makers to develop valuable and beautiful goods and lays the groundwork for creativity and experimentation in this age-old craft.

The Role of Fats, Oils, And Lye

The ancient art of soap-making has developed over many years, emphasizing the relationship between lye, fats, and oils. These essential components undergo a chemical reaction during the saponification process, which is the process of manufacturing soap, to produce the finished washing product. The basis of soap is fats and oils, which give it its hardness, lather, and moisturizing qualities.

Fatty acids comprise the triglycerides that makeup fats and oils, which can come from plants or animals. Every kind of fat or oil has unique qualities that contribute to soap manufacturing. Such as olive oil offers hydrating qualities, and coconut oil helps create a fizzy lather. The final characteristics of the soap, such as its texture, fragrance, and general efficacy, are greatly influenced by the choice and blend of these fats and oils.

In the making of soap, lye, also known as sodium hydroxide, is a potent alkali. In the presence of fats and oils, this caustic substance saponifies the triglycerides, converting them into fatty acids and glycerol. Glycerine and soap are the end products of this chemical process. It is significant to remember that the effectiveness of the soap-making process depends on the precise measurement of lye. If you use too little lye, your soap won't clean your skin well enough, and if you use too much, it will be extremely harsh and irritating.

Glycerine is produced as a byproduct of saponification, which also turns fats and oils into soap. As a naturally occurring humectant, glycerine draws and holds moisture to the skin. This characteristic helps make soap less drying than store-bought equivalents by adding to its moisturizing impact. Glycerine retention enhances the value of handmade soap by providing a more nutritious and skin-friendly washing experience.

The fine art of soap manufacturing is striking the right balance between types and amounts of fats, oils, and lye. Soap makers often experiment with different combinations to attain the required qualities in their soap, such as hardness, lather, cleaning power, and moisturizing effects. Ethics can also play a role in selecting fats and oils; people looking for cruelty-free and environmentally friendly alternatives frequently favor plant-based options.

Mastering the physics underlying soap-making enables craftspeople to make one-of-a-kind, personalized goods that cater to specific requirements and tastes. Soap makers can create soaps appropriate for various skin types, including oily, dry, and sensitive skin, by choosing the fats and oils they use. Since customers value handmade soaps' natural and individualized traits more and more, their popularity has increased due to their formulation's adaptability.

Overall, the base of soap manufacturing is the interaction of fats, oils, and lye. This age-old trade has changed over the years, fusing custom with contemporary knowledge. The craft of picking ingredients and the science of saponification allow soap producers to create a wide variety of soaps with unique qualities. The development of high-quality, nutritious, and efficient cleansing products in soap-making continues to depend heavily on the role of fats, oils, and lye as customers choose natural and customized skincare solutions.

Achieving The Right Balance for A Quality Soap

A thorough understanding of the materials and their balances is necessary for crafting high-quality handcrafted soap. The proper balance must be struck when producing soap that not only cleans the skin but also feeds and pampers it. Fats, oils, and lye are the main ingredients in this alchemical process, and the harmonious combination of these ingredients produces soap of remarkable quality.

Any soap's basis comprises fats and oils; choosing these ingredients is crucial to the soap's final properties. Different oils and fats offer unique properties. In particular, olive oil adds moisturizing qualities, palm oil gives hardness, and coconut oil adds a rich lather. These ingredients need to be carefully selected and blended in order to reach the right balance and produce soap with the correct texture, flavor, and performance.

One cannot stress the importance of lye, or sodium hydroxide, in manufacturing soap. The saponification process, which turns fats and oils into soap, is started by the strong alkali lye. It's a delicate effort to get the ideal lye balance, though. If there is not enough lye, the soap will be too harsh and can irritate the skin, whereas if there is too much lye, the soap won't clean well. Accurate measurements and computations are essential to achieve the ideal balance and guarantee a safe and premium soap.

The art of formulation by the soap maker is more important than the chemical reaction. Experimenting with various ratios of fats, oils, and lye is necessary to create a unique soap. Using a trial-and-error method, craftspeople can perfect their formulas and find the perfect ratio to make soap that reflects their ideas. In addition to smells and colors, creative people also use exfoliants and other substances like herbs to enhance the overall sensory experience of the finished soap.

Suiting different skin types and preferences is critical in striking the proper balance. Since every person is unique, a more than one-size-fits-all strategy might be needed. Craftspeople who create soap frequently focus on crafting bar soaps for particular skin types, like oily, dry, or fragile skin. A careful selection of fats and oils that target specific skincare issues without compromising the soap's general integrity allows this customization.

The formula is not the end of the search for the ideal equilibrium. From the temperature at which components are blended to the soap's curing time, every detail of the soap-making process requires meticulous attention to detail. When manufacturing soap, patience pays off because it improves its hardness, lifespan, and quality when correctly cured. Curing is necessary to turn lye into a mild and harmless chemical that makes the soap skin-friendly.

As individuals become more aware of the items they use, handmade soaps are growing in popularity. Natural, cruelty-free and ecologically friendly solutions are in demand, encouraging makers to hone their skills further. Achieving the ideal balance in handmade soap corresponds with these consumer desires, providing a cleanser and a product that represents a dedication to ethical sourcing, high quality, and a personal touch.

Finally, mastering the skill of striking the perfect balance in handcrafted soap is a complex process that calls for exact measurements, a thorough comprehension of the components, and creative intuition. This intricate ballet of fats, oils, and lye produces a soap that is delightful to the senses and a powerful cleanser. To pay the premium, customized, and decadent handmade soaps, artists in this age-old trade constantly search for the ideal balance.

CHAPTER III

Sustainable Sourcing

Choosing Eco-Friendly and Ethical Ingredients

Choosing eco-friendly and ethical materials is becoming increasingly important in the ever-changing world of homemade soap crafting. The intentional alteration in component selection reflects the soap industry's growing awareness of the moral and ecological consequences of the materials utilized in soap formulations. The choice of ingredients is paramount in the skill of artists who aim to produce goods consistent with sustainable methods.

When making soap by hand, one of the most important factors to consider is the selection of eco-friendly oils. Plant-based oils that are ethically and sustainably sourced, like palm oil that has earned an RSPO certification, are becoming increasingly popular. By maintaining the rights of local communities and workers, preventing deforestation, and minimizing environmental effects, palm oil is produced under the RSPO certification. Shea butter is a moisturizing option that comes from the nuts of the shea tree and is considered environmentally beneficial. Utilizing oils certified by ethical and environmental organizations is in line with the environmental stewardship efforts of the soap-making community.

Handmade soap makers can also add enticing fragrances to their works by using essential oils and fragrance oils in their soap. Plant-based essential oils support environmentally responsible methods while adding to the soap's fragrant appeal. In contrast to synthetic fragrance oils, essential oils are produced using techniques like steam distillation or cold pressing, which minimizes their impact on the environment. Besides their sensual appeal, essential oils frequently have therapeutic qualities that give the soap an additional dimension.

Colorants, a necessary component for making soap, present yet another opportunity for artists to choose environmentally friendly options. Natural colorants made from plants, herbs, and minerals are an environmentally friendly substitute for artificial dyes. Spirulina, turmeric, and clay are among the ingredients that give the soap its colorful hues and health benefits. To help ensure that the soap's aesthetic appeal is attained without compromising environmental sustainability, the eco-friendly philosophy of handcrafted soap manufacture uses natural colorants.

Botanicals and exfoliants added to handmade soap compositions also offer a chance to improve the product's functionality and appearance. Ground coffee, lavender buds, and calendula petals are well-liked options that provide further skin benefits and aesthetic appeal. Choosing botanicals and sustainably supplied exfoliants reduces the environmental impact of their cultivation and harvesting. This thought process indicates a more significant effort on the part of the soap industry to produce opulent yet socially and ecologically conscious goods.

The idea of sustainability applies not only to specific ingredient selections but also to the overall composition of a soap recipe. The secret to creating eco-friendly soap is finding a balance between plentiful, ethically obtained oils and having particular advantages for the skin. By varying their oils, craftspeople can make special mixtures that suit different skin tones and tastes. Shea butter, cocoa butter, and rich oils like coconut and olive add to the richness of the recipe, making the soap both delightful to use and kind to the environment.

The packaging decisions made by artisans also reflect the eco-friendly and ethical nature of the soap they produce. Reducing waste and using eco-friendly packing materials are consistent with the larger goal of lowering the environmental impact of handcrafted soap. Traditional plastic packaging is becoming less and less used in favor of recyclable or biodegradable packaging choices like cardboard or paper. Artisans are investigating cutting-edge methods for displaying and preserving handmade soaps without sacrificing their sustainability commitment.

In addition, there's a growing movement in the community to adopt the zero-waste philosophy when manufacturing soap. Craftspeople are investigating ways to generate new items, such as soap balls or confetti soap, out of leftover soap fragments or flawed batches. By using this method, waste is not only decreased but also the ingenuity and inventiveness of soap makers in identifying environmentally friendly ways to practice their trade.

The eco-friendly technique also considers the amount of water used in soap-making. Craftspeople are becoming more conscious of their water usage even though water is essential to soap-making. Soap production can be made more sustainably by using effective mixing methods, careful pouring, and planning to reduce water waste. This consciousness corresponds with the broader recognition in the artisan soap-making community of the significance of conserving water.

Beyond the particular choices they make about ingredients and packaging, a growing number of soap manufacturers are embracing a broad commitment to ethical and sustainable practices throughout their supply chain. This involves acquiring raw materials from vendors who respect fair labor standards, prioritize treating employees ethically, and make constructive contributions to the communities in which they operate. Artisans are looking for openness in the supply chain to ensure that every ingredient in their formulas complies with ethical norms.

Handmade soap makers are experiencing a paradigm shift due to the eco-friendly and ethical movement. Artists are realizing how much power they have to shape consumer behavior and encourage environmentally friendly lifestyles. An increasingly green-conscious consumer base seeking items that share their beliefs is responding well to this mindset.

Selecting ethical and environmentally friendly ingredients can be a life-changing experience for those who make homemade soap. Dedication to ethical and environmental principles is evident in every choice, from sustainably sourced essential oils to natural colorants, botanicals, and eco-friendly packaging. Since soap makers work together to make these environmentally responsible decisions, the industry benefits from a more significant trend toward sustainable and ethical consumption.

Supporting Local and Fair-Trade Suppliers

Making handmade soap is more than an artistic endeavor; it's a journey that penetrates communities and economies beyond the soap-making facility. Deliberately sourcing the necessary ingredients for a soap recipe from local and fair-trade suppliers is becoming increasingly popular among soap makers. This dedication aligns with a larger philosophy of sustainability, moral production, and community development that appeals to customers and artists.

Choosing oils is one of the most essential components of homemade soap, and going with locally produced and fairly traded products may make a big difference. Local oils from farmers or farms can lower the transportation sector's carbon footprint. Local artists frequently establish direct connections that promote accountability and community when they interact with oil producers. Since the sourcing process is transparent, artists can track the origin of their oils and make sure they meet environmental and ethical criteria.

Fair-trade methods further enhance the advantages of obtaining ingredients for handcrafted soap. Fair-trade certification fosters just and long-lasting commercial partnerships by guaranteeing that producers, frequently found in developing countries, are fairly compensated for their goods. Soap makers actively participate in a global movement emphasizing social responsibility by actively searching for fair-trade oils. This dedication goes beyond the simple trade of manufacturing soap; it becomes a modest but significant effort to fight poverty and uplift local communities everywhere.

Including botanicals, herbs, and other natural additions alongside the oils distinguishes handmade soap making. Artists committed to supporting their community's economy frequently investigate the abundance of native plants and herbs in their area. Sourcing these plants locally encourages a feeling of connectedness to the natural world while promoting biodiversity in the area. Getting to know local herbalists or going on a foraging expedition for native plants merges the art of soap-making with the preservation of regional ecosystems comprehensively and sustainably.

Obtaining scents for handcrafted soap is included in supporting local suppliers, not just for botanicals. Producers frequently work with regional perfumers or essential oil distillers to produce signature aromas that embody the area's spirit. This customized technique honors the richness of the local environment's scents while giving the soap a distinctive touch. In addition, interacting with neighborhood fragrance providers forges stronger bonds throughout the community and fosters a win-win partnership in which the local supplier and the soap maker prosper.

Finding ingredients and packaging materials is as important as selecting local and fair-trade vendors. Artisans concerned about the environment frequently look for eco-friendly packaging choices from nearby vendors. Packaging materials supplied locally, like cardboard or recycled paper, help lessen the environmental effect of shipping. This method contributes to the larger philosophy of reducing the ecological impact of handmade soap, producing a skin-nourishing product that simultaneously shows a dedication to environmental care.

In light of the economic and social aspects of soap making, the dedication to assisting fair-trade and local vendors becomes even greater significant. Regional manufacturers support the development of jobs and long-term economic viability. Artists, by using local suppliers, support the growth of local companies in their communities. This interconnected web of support strengthens the economic fabric, which has an impact well beyond the specific art of soap-making.

Moreover, the focus on fair-trade methods encourages moral production standards, guaranteeing that all parties in the supply chain receive equitable treatment. Fairtrade is based on the fundamental tenet of paying farmers, laborers, and suppliers fairly; soap makers that share this philosophy become social justice activists. Fair-trade policies impact the lives of people and communities involved in producing raw materials, and their effects go beyond the soap-making workshop.

Also, promoting regional and fair-trade producers is in line with customers' growing need for goods that are made in an ethical and socially conscious manner. An increasing number of consumers are increasingly conscious of the ethical consequences of the products they purchase, which makes handmade soap made with fair-trade and locally sourced ingredients all the more appealing. This appeals to customers looking for skincare products that demonstrate a dedication to sustainable living and global citizenship. Artisans who prioritize supporting local and fair-trade suppliers often find themselves at the intersection of craftsmanship and community engagement. Local farmers, producers, and suppliers become integral partners in the soap-making process, and the relationships formed go beyond mere transactions. The stories behind the ingredients become woven into the soap narrative, enriching the artisan's connection to their craft and the communities that contribute to its vitality.

Supporting regional and fair-trade vendors has a knock-on impact that extends into the larger ethical consumer narrative. As customers get pickier about the goods they purchase, the soap maker becomes a change agent in the crafting community. Decisions about the source of ingredients and packaging materials convey an important message of accountability, responsibility, and dedication to making a positive difference in the world.

Ultimately, choosing to support fair-trade and local vendors when manufacturing handmade soap is a decision that has a profound impact beyond the soap studio. Incorporating sustainability, ethics, and community empowerment into the craft's design is a deliberate choice. Manufacturers that embrace this attitude become ambassadors for a soap-making community that values the beauty of their creations but also the interrelated well-being of the global community. Examples of this community's products include locally sourced oils and botanicals, fair-trade procedures that encourage equitable partnerships, and more.

Reducing Environmental Impact in The Sourcing Process

As the artisanal soap-making community becomes more committed to sustainable practices and awareness, it is clear that limiting the environmental impact of the sourcing process is a crucial part of crafting handcrafted soap. The choice and sourcing of raw materials, such as oils, additives, and packaging, are all part of the sourcing process, which is crucial in establishing the total environmental impact of handcrafted soap. In an effort to make their craft in line with environmentally conscious values, craftsmen go into the complexities of sourcing, tracking every component from the point of origin to the point of manufacturing to make sure it has a positive environmental impact.

The careful selection of oils is the foundation of manufacturing soap that is environmentally conscientious. There has been a notable change in the market, with consumers favoring oils that are ethically sourced and sustainably produced. This change has focused on palm oil, a commonly used product, because of worries about habitat degradation and deforestation. An increasing number of artisans are choosing to utilize palm oil that has undergone certification from the Roundtable on Palm Oil Sustainability to ensure that their product satisfies the strictest social and environmental standards. This accreditation reflects a dedication to lowering the environmental effect of palm oil sourcing by emphasizing ethical labor standards, wildlife conservation, and appropriate growing methods.

The larger goal of lessening environmental effect is furthered by buying oils from regional and fair-trade sources. Because oils purchased closer to the soap-making location need less travel time and associated greenhouse gas emissions, local sourcing reduces the carbon footprint associated with transportation.

Supporting neighborhood vendors also encourages community involvement and contributes to the development of robust local economies. Craftspeople are realizing more and more how vital it is to build linkages with adjacent producers, guarantee openness in the sourcing procedure, and support the long-term viability of their industry and surrounding communities.

The sourcing of different ingredients for soap-making is becoming more and more aligned with fair-trade norms. Ingredients from areas with great biodiversity and indigenous communities are frequently the source of ingredients like shea butter, cocoa butter, and unusual oils. Adopting fair-trade principles promotes social well-being and economic empowerment by ensuring that these communities are fairly compensated for their resources.

In order to provide customers peace of mind that their soap is made ethically, artisans proactively pursue fair-trade certificates for their raw materials. The process of sourcing botanicals and additives for handmade soap is another avenue where environmental impact can be reduced. Botanicals, such as herbs and flowers, add aesthetic and therapeutic value to soap. Sourcing these botanicals from local and sustainable suppliers promotes biodiversity conservation and minimizes the ecological impact associated with harvesting practices.

Implementing ethical and sustainable harvesting methods ensures that the use of botanicals does not compromise the natural ecosystems they are sourced from, contributing to the preservation of plant diversity.

Acquiring oils from fair-trade and local suppliers advances the overall objective of reducing the impact on the environment. Local sourcing lowers the transportation-related carbon footprint since oils bought closer to the soap-making facility require less travel time and related greenhouse gas emissions. Encouraging neighborhood sellers also helps to build strong local economies and fosters community involvement. Craftsmen are becoming increasingly aware of how important it is to establish connections with neighboring producers, ensure transparency in the sourcing process, and promote the long-term health of their sector and the communities in which they operate.

The source of various materials for soap production is increasingly following fair-trade guidelines. Ingredients like exotic oils, cocoa butter, and shea butter are frequently obtained from areas with significant indigenous people and biodiversity. Adopting fair-trade principles guarantees that these communities receive just compensation for their resources, which in turn fosters social well-being and economic empowerment. For their raw materials, craftsmen actively seek fair-trade certifications, giving consumers the assurance that their soap is produced responsibly.

Reducing environmental effects is further enhanced by using a zero-waste strategy in the sourcing process. Throughout the soap-making process, artisans look for creative methods to make the most out of leftovers. Practices that demonstrate a dedication to sustainability include upcycling soap scraps into new goods, making confetti soaps, and recycling defective batches. This zero-waste approach reduces environmental impact while also showcasing the ingenuity and skill of soap makers in incorporating eco-friendly solutions into their art.

The procurement of water, a vital component in the production of soap, is subject to examination in the endeavor to mitigate ecological footprints. Even though water is necessary to make soap, craftspeople are starting to use water-saving techniques more and more. Making soap is a more sustainable process when it involves effective mixing methods, careful pouring, and planning to use as little extra water as possible. This thoughtful approach is consistent with the industry's wider recognition of the value of water conservation among makers of artisan soap.

Additionally, one of the most important factors in sourcing and production is lowering the energy usage during the soap-making process. Energy-intensive techniques, like producing soap in the hot process, could leave a bigger environmental impact. Alternative techniques, such as cold process soap manufacturing, which uses less energy and is in line with environmentally friendly principles, are investigated by artisans. Reducing environmental effects is furthered by implementing energy-efficient technologies and practices in the soap-making workspace, such as employing renewable energy sources or natural light.

One component of making handcrafted soap that is constantly changing is the sourcing process, which reflects the artists' ongoing dedication to lessening their environmental impact. The transition in sourcing tactics towards eco-friendly and sustainable methods is a true acknowledgment by the soap-making community of the connection between their art and the environment, as well as a reaction to customer demand for ethical products. Craftsmen who successfully negotiate the challenges of sourcing are part of a broader trend in the handmade soap market that places emphasis on ethical behavior, environmental awareness, and the long-term sustainability of the craft.

CHAPTER IV

Artistic Approaches to Soap Crafting

Various Soap-Making Techniques (Cold Process, Hot Process, Melt and Pour)

Manufacturing soap is a centuries-old craft that has evolved into a diverse art form with various applications to fit a range of skill levels, preferences, and creative expressions. The Cold Process (CP), Hot Process (HP), and Melt and Pour (MP) procedures are widely used, and each contributes distinct qualities to the handmade soap industry.

The Cold Process is one of the oldest and most fundamental techniques for creating soap. This method starts saponification by mixing oils and fats with a sodium hydroxide (lye) solution. The ability to provide soap manufacturers with a great deal of control over ingredients and design sets CP apart. This technique offers various creative possibilities by incorporating different oils, butter, and additions. The creative freedom that CP provides to soap crafters is widely appreciated, as it enables them to explore complex swirls, patterns, and color combinations. One benefit of CP is its lengthy drying time, which helps to create a smooth and refined result. Although the soap may take a few weeks to months to cure, the finished product is typically mild, hydrating, and attractive.

On the other hand, the Hot Process is characterized by applying heat to accelerate the saponification process. This process combines oils with lye, which is heated to speed up the chemical reaction. As a result, soap makers can now produce their finished goods in a matter of days instead of weeks. Because of its faster production process, HP soap tends to seem more rustic. The heat used during the process affects the soap's texture, making it less smooth than CP soap. Even though HP's design may not be as intricate as CP's, it is nevertheless a well-liked option for people who prioritize speed and efficiency when creating soap. Furthermore, soap producers can test and use their creations sooner due to the shortened curing time.

On the other hand, Melt and Pour, which uses pre-made soap bases, is a very beginner-friendly method. Once these bases are melted, soap manufacturers can add different ingredients, like colorants, perfumes, and exfoliants. The melt-and-pour method appeals to novice soap makers since it does not require lye, which removes the risk of handling this corrosive material. MP is praised for its ease of use and speedy outcomes; producers can have completed, usable soaps in hours. Melt and Pour is a great way to get started in soap crafting and offers a creative platform for experimenting, even though it might not give you as much control over the ingredients as CP or HP.

When selecting among these methods, the soap maker's tastes, experience, and intended results are generally considered. Some artists focus on a single technique, becoming masters in it and refining their works accordingly. Conversely, some individuals use a blend of approaches, capitalizing on each methodology's distinct advantages.

The adaptability and imaginative potential of the cold process make it highly valued. Soap manufacturers commonly employ a range of oils, such as olive, coconut, palm, and shea butter, to make personalized soaps for various skin types. Due to CP's slow tracing feature, artists may create complex swirls, layers, and motifs. This process is a perfect fit for natural colorants like clays, botanicals, and essential oils, which enhance the soap's skin-friendly qualities and visual attractiveness. CP fans also value their control over super-fatting, which is the addition of extra fats that aren't saponified but still add moisture to the soap.

Efficiency-seekers don't have to sacrifice quality for faster saponification while creating soap with the hot process. People who want a quicker turnaround time will find this strategy especially intriguing. HP lovers appreciate the earthy and textured appeal that the rustic appearance imparts, even though it may not have the refined finish of CP soap. Heat guarantees that the soap is completely saponified during the cooking process, obviating the need for a protracted curing time. To enhance the strong qualities of hot process soap, soap producers frequently experiment with different fragrances and colorants.

Crafting is a great place to start for those who want to enjoy the artistic side of soap making without having to deal with lye, melt, and pour soap. Melting a pre-made soap base and adding additions to customize it is the process. Melt & Pour aficionados can create aesthetically pleasing and fragrant soaps by experimenting with colors, fragrances, and embeds. This technique is well-liked for making novelty soaps, themed crafts, or personalized presents. Melt and Pour is a popular alternative for various soap-making tasks because of its ease and speedy turnaround, even though it may not have as many ingredient options as CP or HP.

Combining different processes is a common source of inspiration for artisans, demonstrating the diversity of soap making. For example, a soap maker might use the cold process to generate a base, then insert slices of a colorful melt and pour soap into it. This combination gives the soap a layer of complexity and permits the creation of elaborate designs. Similarly, some soap producers use a hybrid technique, starting with a hot process and adding cold components for aesthetics.

Ultimately, handcrafted soap production is thriving due to the diverse methods employed, with popular approaches like Melt and Pour, Hot Process, and Cold Process each having distinct advantages. The selection of these methods is contingent upon various elements, including aesthetic inclinations, degree of expertise, temporal limitations, and intended results. Many soap makers enjoy pushing the limits of creativity and skill within the soap-making community by experimenting with the many possibilities these techniques offer.

Using Colors, Fragrances, and Additives

Soap makers use a wide range of colors, scents, and additives to enhance their creations, demonstrating the artistic side of the craft that goes beyond the basic components of oils and lye. Producing soap becomes a visually interesting experience when colors are used, enabling makers to add color, creativity, and a hint of luxury to their creations. Blending earthy tones and delicate hues, natural colorants including clays, herbal infusions, and powdered botanicals offer a healthy substitute for artificial dyes. Made from minerals, Mica powders add glimmer and shine to the soap, improving its visual appeal. By carefully choosing and combining colorants, soap makers can create designs with a particular theme, inspire particular moods, or highlight the inherent beauty of the materials.

Fragrances are Essential to producing soap, which arouse the sense of smell and enhance the whole sensory experience. Plant-based essential oils come in a wide range of fragrances, from the energizing whiff of citrus to the relaxing undertones of lavender. Fragrance oils, frequently made synthetically, offer various choices, including intricate mixtures replicating well-known odors. The selection of fragrances enables soap manufacturers to create soaps that address particular inclinations, events, or medicinal goals. Soaps with lavender extract, for instance, might be made to help people unwind and reduce tension, and combinations of citrus energy can stimulate the senses. When soap makers use, fragrance can arouse feelings, take consumers to new places, and increase their overall enjoyment.

In addition to color and fragrance, a variety of other ingredients can influence the feel, texture, and skin-beneficial properties of the finished soap. In addition to adding visual appeal, botanicals like dried herbs, flowers, and seeds give the soap exfoliating qualities. Ground coffee and oats offer a mild exfoliation that encourages skin renewal and a refreshed appearance. Clays are renowned for their cleansing and purifying properties and help create a rich, creamy lather. Furthermore, adding ingredients like honey or silk fibers can improve the soap's hydrating and silky qualities, giving the skin a caressing feeling.

Activated charcoal is a highly sought-after ingredient for detoxifying soaps since it not only adds a stunning black color but also pulls pollutants from the skin. Specialty oils, such as jojoba or argan oil, also add decadence and help hydrate and nourish the body. The world of soap additions is a world of infinite possibilities, where makers can play around with textures, add natural materials, and customize their compositions to meet certain skin demands.

Soap producers need to comprehend the characteristics of different additions to produce a well-rounded and efficient product. For example, adding menthol crystals to the soap can give it a pleasant, cooling feel, but using it too often could irritate your skin. Similarly, adding sea salt can help create a bar that is tougher and lasts longer in addition to adding texture. The right balance of additive amounts, compatibility, and potential benefits guarantee that the soap not only smells and looks good, but also gives the user a healthy and pleasurable experience.

Creating soap is a creative process that frequently involves a subtle dance between color, scent, and ingredients, each adding something unique to the finished product. Artists may decide to arrange these elements in a way that develops a unified subject, or they may decide to develop a contrast that appeals to several senses at once. For instance, a relaxation-focused soap might have calming scents like eucalyptus or chamomile and colors like lavender or pastel blues. On the other hand, an energetic soap can include vivid citrus colors, stimulating scents like orange or lemon, and exfoliating ingredients that stimulate the senses.

These components also extend to the layering technique, in which soap artisans employ a single mold to generate multiple-colored layers for visual interest. This process enables the creation of complicated gradients or patterns in the soap, exhibiting an eye-catching degree of intricacy and detail. Another inventive technique is embedding, which is putting smaller, shaped pieces inside the soap to give a surprise factor when the soap is used and the embedded pieces come to light.

The discovery of novel and unusual ingredients has emerged as a characteristic of the trade as soapmaking continues to develop. For example, beer soap offers a distinctive twist by adding more sugars, amino acids, and minerals to the soap batter by using beer. A similar idea is used with wine soap, which imbues the soap with the flavors and rich colors of the selected wine. Due to its exfoliating qualities, coffee grounds are frequently used to make exfoliating scrubs that leave the skin feeling revitalized and slightly rough. These imaginative projects show the room for creativity in the soap-making industry.

The creative freedom that colors, scents, and additions provide, however, also presents obstacles for soap makers when using particular components. Certain essential oils or perfumes can cause allergies and sensitivities, therefore ingredient lists need to be transparent so that customers can make educated decisions. Furthermore, one must be mindful of the environmental effects while procuring specific compounds, especially those from exotic or endangered species. In the soap-making community, sustainable and ethical methods encompass the careful choice of materials and a dedication to ethical sourcing, waste minimization, and a reduction in the craft's overall ecological imprint.

Finally, adding colors, scents, and additions to soap creates a sensory experience that elevates the art form. Inspired by a strong desire to improve the user experience and a passion for creativity, soap artists work through a wide range of options. Handmade soap crafting is a dynamic and multi-dimensional art form constantly evolving. From the visual appeal of carefully chosen colorants to the aromatic delight of carefully picked aromas and the textural richness of varied ingredients, there is always more to discover. The industry that produces soap is paving the way for a day when soap is not only a daily treat for the senses but also an innovation, sustainability, and well-being of the consumer.

Creating Unique Designs and Patterns

Producing soap is a craft that is both practical and expressive, allowing for personal expression and creativity. Developing unique designs and motifs has become a fascinating facet of the industry, wherein craftsmen turn plain bars into eye-catching creations. The soap maker's imagination is the limit regarding design possibilities, and the methods used range from deft swirls and layering to embedding and sculpting.

The swirl method, which is frequently connected to the cold process, is one of the essential methods for creating eye-catching designs in soap. Carefully blending several colored soap batters, soap artists pour the mixture into a mold and use various swirling techniques to produce captivating designs. As a result, a soap that resembles delicate galaxies or marbled patterns is complex and intriguing. There are several options, ranging from the traditional hanger swirl to more complex methods like the mantra swirl or butterfly swirl, which all require high skill, accuracy, and aesthetic sensibility.

Another well-liked method for producing aesthetically attractive bars with several colored or textured levels is layering. Artists can produce a dynamic and three-dimensional look by layering varied amounts of soap batter into a mold and waiting for each layer to solidify before adding the next. In addition to being aesthetically pleasing, layering allows for incorporating various ingredients, colors, and smells into each layer, creating a sensory experience that changes with each use.

A creative and unexpected touch is added when items are embedded in soap. Artisans can place tiny objects such as flowers, herbs, or even tiny soap shapes strategically inside the soap mold. These embedded elements become visible as the soap cures and is cut into separate bars, producing a stunning sight. Soap manufacturers can include narrative or theme components to their works by embedding, which offers countless customization and personalization options.

Soap carving and molding provide a more sculptural method for creating elaborate, three-dimensional motifs. Bars are shaped and carved into complex designs, forms, and even sculptures by soap carvers using tools. Due to the precision and attention to detail required for soap carving, this approach calls for a combination of ability and patience. On the other hand, molding entails making unique molds to form the soap into certain shapes. With the help of this process, craftspeople can create soap bars in various forms, such as intricate copies of things or symbols or geometric patterns.

Using sophisticated techniques like the Taiwan swirl or drop swirl demonstrates the soap-making community's depth of expertise and mastery. These methods entail pouring soap batter from an elevated position or applying particular pouring techniques to produce elaborate designs in the soap. For example, the drop swirl generates an enthralling waterfall of colors, while the Taiwan swirl makes a lovely flower-like design. The skill of creating soap is constantly evolving, pushing the limits of what is conceivable in terms of design and aesthetic appeal, as craftspeople investigate and disseminate these cutting-edge methods.

Furthermore, adding organic components to soap designs—like botanicals and exfoliants—brings further visual appeal and practicality. It is possible to add strategically placed dried flowers, herbs, or seeds to the soap, improving its appearance and offering further skin benefits and exfoliating qualities. Soap makers can create visually striking bars that celebrate the beauty of nature by carefully arranging these materials.

Many artistic disciplines, such as painting, sculpture, and culinary arts, inspire soap manufacturers. Methods like "in-the-pot swirl" and "brush embroidery" are similar to painting in that both involve using tools to produce complex patterns or replicate the brushstrokes of a painting. Like sculpture, soap makers can approach soap creation as a three-dimensional art form through layering and sculpting. Creative influences interacting with one another creates a dynamic, ever-changing soap design.

Achieving aesthetically pleasing designs in soapmaking greatly depends on the color selection. Soap producers can achieve vast colors without artificial dyes by utilizing natural colorants like mica, clays, and powdered botanicals. Every colorant has distinct qualities, such as mica's shimmering effects or clays' earthy tones. Soap artists can express particular themes or moods through thoughtful color selection and blending. The color wheel is a tool used by soap manufacturers to generate visually appealing and harmonious combinations, whether they are going for a bright explosion of colors or a soothing pallet of pastels.

Scents enhance soap's visual appeal and contribute significantly to its entire sensory experience. The theme or design concept of the soap is frequently linked to the fragrance selection. The thematic coherence of a soap with flower motifs, for instance, could be strengthened by the use of smells like rose or lavender. The skillful blending of scents and colors provides the user with a comprehensive and immersive experience.

Moreover, using ingredients such as moisturizing agents or exfoliants affects the soap's appearance and performance. In addition to adding visually appealing patterns, carefully positioned seeds, oats, or coffee grounds inside the soap also offer textural interest and exfoliation. On the other hand, moisturizing ingredients like glycerine or shea butter can affect the look and feel of the soap, giving it a luscious and velvety appearance.

Within the active and cooperative soap-making community, craftspeople freely share their discoveries, designs, and techniques. Online forums, social media groups, and platforms act as virtual hubs where enthusiasts can interact, share ideas, and show off their achievements. This sense of community encourages a culture of ongoing experimentation and learning, advancing soap design.

Although there are many opportunities in soap production, there are also difficulties, especially when it comes to using certain chemicals, considering the environment, and sourcing ethically. To overcome these obstacles, soap manufacturers prioritize formulation transparency, use sustainable processes, and choose components supplied ethically. A thoughtful and socially conscious community is further enhanced by the growing understanding of the benefits of producing soap ethically and ecologically sustainably.

Conclusively, the art form of soap production that goes beyond the practical parts of the craft is the creation of distinctive designs and patterns. The creativity, self-expression, and desire to provide customers with a multisensory experience inspire soap artists to always push the limits of what is possible with the material. Combining different methods, hues, scents, and additions results in soap bars that are both aesthetically pleasing and functionally rewarding. There will always be room for more research, experimentation, and producing genuinely exceptional soaps because the soap-making community is built on cooperation, creativity, and a passion for the art.

CHAPTER V

Crafting Specialty Soaps

Organic And Natural Soap Variations

Handmade soap, a timeless craft that has grown in popularity, stands at the intersection of art and science. Within this artisanal realm, the demand for organic and natural soap variations has gained considerable momentum, reflecting a broader societal shift towards conscious consumerism and a desire for products aligned with nature. Organic and natural soaps are distinct categories within handmade soap crafting, embodying specific principles, ingredients, and production methods that resonate with individuals seeking a closer connection to nature and a commitment to environmental sustainability.

Organic soap, as the name suggests, is crafted using certified organic ingredients. The term "organic" refers to the farming and cultivation methods employed for the raw materials involved in soap making. Organic farming eschews synthetic pesticides, herbicides, and fertilizers, emphasizing natural processes to enhance soil fertility and biodiversity. This translates to using oils, butters, and botanicals sourced from organically grown plants in soap crafting. Organic substances such as olive oil, coconut oil, shea butter, and essential oils made from organic plants are frequently used when producing soap.

According to the strict guidelines established by organic certifying authorities, organic soap must pass certification. By following these guidelines, you may be sure that every item satisfies certain requirements, such as not containing GMOs (genetically modified organisms) and being produced without artificial chemicals. Manufacturers of soap dedicated to creating organic soaps frequently undergo the difficult certification procedure, giving customers confidence about the veracity of their organic claims. The end product is a soap that emphasizes sustainability, healthy soil, and the health of ecosystems while also cleaning and adhering to organic agricultural principles.

Conversely, natural soap is a more inclusive category that includes various components obtained straight from nature. Natural soap does not always meet the strict requirements needed to receive an organic certification, even though it might include some organic components. With ingredients like botanicals, clays, and minerals, natural soap takes a holistic approach to offering a sensory experience rooted in the abundance of nature. Utilizing minimally processed, plant-based components, the goal is to make a soap that evokes the simplicity and purity of the natural world for its customers.

The lack of artificial colorants, perfumes, and additives is one of the characteristics that distinguish both natural and organic soaps. Rather, these soaps' color, scent, and medicinal properties come from the natural properties of plant-based components. Natural colorants like clays, herbs, and spices imparted Earthy hues into the soap. Additionally, essential oils derived from plants offer appealing fragrances and possibly even therapeutic benefits. These components improve the bathing experience and enhance the soap's visual beauty.

Individual priorities and tastes often influence the decision between natural and organic soaps. Some customers place a high value on certified organic products because they appreciate the stringent adherence to organic standards. The genuineness and simplicity of natural soaps may satisfy others just as much, who will value their reliance on minimally processed components without the certification requirements. Transparency, sustainability, and a stronger relationship to the soap's ingredient sources are the essential tenets in both situations.

Various variations and specialty formulations have arisen within organic and natural soaps that address various skin types, preferences, and wellness goals. Hypoallergenic versions of organic and natural soaps are made carefully to select suitable ingredients for people with sensitive skin. Sweet almond, avocado, and olive oil are mild, skin-nourishing oils that frequently take center stage and offer a mild washing experience free of harsh chemicals or other allergens.

Additionally, specialty soaps with specific benefits have grown in popularity in the market for organic and natural soaps. Herbal-infused soaps, for instance, might contain plants with calming and soothing effects on the skin, including lavender, calendula, or chamomile. Variations on exfoliation might include natural ingredients like oatmeal, coffee grinds, or sea salt, which work as a mild scrub to encourage skin rejuvenation. Adding particular essential oils selected for their aromatherapeutic properties gives the bathing routine a new depth. It transforms into a sensory treat that benefits the body and the mind.

The popularity of Ayurvedic and herbal soap formulations is a noteworthy subcategory among organic and natural soap options. These soaps combine the concepts of Ayurveda or herbal medicine with traditional healing practices to develop mixtures that address specific skin conditions. Ingredients including neem, tulsi, and turmeric—known in Ayurvedic traditions for their purifying, antimicrobial, and skin-balancing qualities— may be found in Ayurvedic soaps. Beyond Ayurveda, the herbal method is used by soap makers, who use a wide variety of plants with well-established health benefits, such as chamomile to ease inflammation or rosemary to promote circulation.

Beyond emphasizing botanical ingredients, creating organic and natural soaps frequently includes eco-friendliness and sustainability. By using sustainably sourced oils and butters, artisans dedicated to environmental stewardship can support programs like fair trade and sustainable farming methods. Furthermore, initiatives to cut packaging's waste and environmental impact are consistent with the conscious consumerism philosophy of the natural and organic soap industry. A commitment to zero-waste methods and the use of recyclable or biodegradable packaging materials both improve the overall sustainability of the handmade soap sector.

Certain soap makers go beyond creating typical bar soaps and provide a variety of natural and organic options to promote authenticity and holistic well-being. Liquid soaps are a practical and adaptable choice for everyday cleaning, frequently made with organic oils and botanical extracts. Specialty formulas, such face cleansers and shampoo bars, address certain skincare requirements without sacrificing their adherence to organic and natural principles. These variations give customers more options that fit their values and interests, expanding the possibilities in manufacturing organic and natural soap. As

people's lifestyles become more conscientious and seek items that align with sustainability and wellbeing, there is a growing interest in natural and organic soaps. The need for authenticity and transparency in soap manufacture keeps the craft's innovation flowing forward as consumers become increasingly picky about the ingredients they expose their skin to. This movement is led by the artisanal soap-making community, distinguished by its inventiveness, dedication to quality, and environmental awareness. This group is reshaping the skincare industry with its organic and natural soap varieties, which highlight the wonders and usefulness of nature's offerings.

Allergen-Free and Sensitive Skin Formulations

Creating formulas specifically for sensitive and allergy-free skin has become a small but important part of the complex world of soap production, where science and creativity collide. Because more people are becoming aware of skin sensitivities and allergies, there is a growing need for soaps that cater to certain skin needs. Since sensitive skin types frequently respond negatively to standard soap ingredients, softness and hypoallergenic qualities should be given priority in soap compositions. These specialty soaps are designed to cleanse without irritating, providing a relief for people dealing with the intricacies of skincare due to increased sensitivity.

Formulations for sensitive and allergy-free skin are based on the thoughtful selection of substances that reduce the possibility of irritation and allergic responses. Fragrance oils, colorants, and preservatives are common components of traditional soap formulas that may trigger sensitization for some skin types. As a result, soap producers have resorted to a more straightforward strategy, concentrating on a small number of pure and hypoallergenic ingredients to produce soaps that effectively cleanse. Because of its mild and moisturizing qualities, olive oil often takes center stage in these products, offering a delicately balanced, gently cleaning basis.

Also, common allergens including nut oils, soy, gluten, and dairy derivatives are usually excluded from allergen-free soaps; nonetheless, these substances can still react negatively to certain people. Since these allergens aren't present, there's less chance of skin irritation, which makes these formulations appropriate for a wider range of consumers. Essential oils are selected with care to ensure they are hypoallergenic and provide a light scent without causing skin irritation. These formulas frequently include essential oils like lavender, chamomile, and calendula, which are well-known for their relaxing and skin-soothing qualities.

Unscented and colorless formulations are vital for people with sensitive skin diseases like dermatitis or eczema. With no possible allergens, these uncomplicated soaps concentrate on the purest and most basic components. These soap formulations commonly include shea butter, which is well-known for its nourishing and moisturizing qualities. This adds to the soap's mildness and skin-friendliness. This washing process aims to ensure that the health and comfort of delicate skin are the first priority while maintaining efficacy.

The cold process method, which guarantees the retention of glycerine, a naturally occurring result of the saponification process, and provides for better control over ingredients, is frequently used by soap producers specializing in formulating for sensitive skin. Humectant glycerine draws moisture to the skin and helps keep it hydrated. Glycerin is frequently eliminated from commercial soap production. Still, when making soaps for delicate skin, it becomes essential to keep this important ingredient to keep skin hydrated and avoid dryness.

The pH level of the soap is an essential factor to consider in formulations for sensitive skin, in addition to the selection of oils and the removal of possible allergens. Since the skin's pH is naturally slightly acidic, soaps that go too far from this range risk upsetting the skin's protective layer, which can cause irritation and dryness. This is something that soap makers consider when creating their products, making sure that the pH remains somewhat near to that of the skin. Allergen-free and sensitive skin soaps are often skin-friendly because of this delicate balancing act.

Regarding hypoallergenic soap recipes, the lack of artificial scents becomes a distinguishing feature. Many different substances found in synthetic perfumes can potentially irritate skin that is already sensitive. Rather than using artificial fragrances, soap makers use natural essential oils to add delicate scents without running the danger of irritating allergies. There are also many options without fragrances for people who want the purest, most fundamental experience with soap. The goal is to make a soap that serves as a ritual of care and comfort for those with sensitive skin as much as a cleansing agent.

Beyond the selection of ingredients, manufacturers of soaps specifically formulated for sensitive skin frequently take an open stance regarding product labeling. Consumers may make educated decisions based on their sensitivities and allergies when they can access clear and comprehensive ingredient lists. The relationship between the soap manufacturer and the customer is strengthened by this transparency, which is based on shared dedication to skin health and accountability. The growing need for soaps free of allergens and suitable for sensitive skin drives home the importance of transparency as a fundamental aspect of the art.

Artisans soap producers have embraced ethical sourcing and sustainability in pursuing skin-friendly compositions. The choice of components takes social duty and environmental responsibility into account in addition to their effect on skin health. For instance, selecting sustainable palm oil demonstrates a dedication to environmentally responsible practices by guaranteeing that the source of components does not lead to deforestation or harm to biodiversity. Customers looking for solutions that not only take care of their skin but also demonstrate a more comprehensive understanding of environmental and social repercussions find resonance in ethical choices made while selecting ingredients.

Experimentation and adaption are constant steps in the delicate dance of formulating for sensitive skin. To improve their formulations, soap manufacturers in this category frequently work with dermatologists, skincare specialists, and people with sensitive skin. The objective is to produce soaps that are not only free of allergens but also offer noticeable advantages for skin health. It is ensured that the process of creating soap is dynamic and responsive to the changing demands of the community of people with sensitive skin by incorporating feedback from people with sensitivities.

Personalization becomes important when manufacturing soap for those with allergies or sensitivity to particular substances. Handcrafted soap manufacturers frequently provide customized choices, enabling clients to ask for adjustments to basic formulas to meet their specific requirements. In addition to satisfying personal preferences, this degree of personalization promotes inclusivity among the soap-making community. It shows a dedication to appreciating and respecting the variety of skin tones, ensuring everyone has access to a soap that meets their needs.

The market for soaps for sensitive skin free of allergens is growing as the trend toward living a more mindful and clean lifestyle gets traction. People are looking for more items that reflect their ideals; this also applies to skincare options. The emergence of artisanal soap producers with small batches that focus on creating products for delicate skin indicates a larger trend toward conscientious consumption. Along with prioritizing skin health, consumers are now taking the ethics and environmental effects of the goods they use daily into account.

In summary, within the larger field of handmade soap making, formulating allergen-free and sensitive skin soaps is a specific craft. This niche's soap makers employ a distinctive fusion of scientific accuracy and creative sensibility to produce compositions that put skin health first without sacrificing the craft's visual or sensory elements. Transparency, sustainability, and customization are prioritized because they demonstrate a dedication to fulfilling the various requirements of people with sensitivities and cultivating an inclusive community that prioritizes skin health. The future looks bright for creative formulas that satisfy the growing need of consumers for skincare products based on the ideals of care, simplicity, and purity as this market continues to develop.

Herbal And Aromatherapy-Infused Soaps

The union of herbal and aromatherapy-infused soaps bears witness to the union of nature's abundance and the craftsmanship of fragrance in the captivating realm of handmade soap making. These soaps are more than just a practical way to clean; they are an all-encompassing sensory experience that benefits the body and mind. Herbal and aromatherapy-infused soaps incorporate the healing qualities of plants and essential oils into the soap-making process, drawing inspiration from the age-old traditions of herbalism and aromatherapy. The end product is a beautifully balanced combination of nature's therapeutic gifts in a bar of soap that cleans the skin and acts as a medium for rest, renewal, and sensory pleasure.

Appreciating plants' therapeutic qualities is at the core of soaps infused with herbs. With its origins firmly established in conventional medicine, herbalism honors the wide range of botanicals that provide numerous skin-benefiting properties. Soap producers use herbs and plant materials for their therapeutic properties and aesthetic appeal. Because of its calming and anti-inflammatory qualities, calendula is sometimes used in formulations for sensitive or inflamed skin. Because of its relaxing and stress-relieving qualities, lavender is a common ingredient in soaps that promote relaxation. Rosemary, prized for its stimulating and circulatory-enhancing properties, gives some formulas a rejuvenating edge.

Herbal-infused soaps use aromatherapy, an alternative that uses plant-based fragrant molecules to improve physical and emotional health. The aromatic characteristic that sets these soaps apart from the norm is essential oils, which are harvested from different portions of plants. Renowned for its calming effects, lavender essential oil transforms cleaning into a peaceful ritual by creating a spa-like ambiance in the shower or bathtub. Citrus oils, including those from orange or bergamot, energize and revitalize the senses while elevating the mood. The thoughtful selection and blending of essential oils enable soap manufacturers to create scents that address particular needs, such as promoting relaxation, renewal, or a sensory experience.

Plant materials and essential oils are carefully blended throughout soap-making to create herbal and aromatherapy-infused soaps. These specialty soaps are typically made using the cold process method, which preserves the natural oils and gives the maker more control over the ingredients. Herbs can be added for their therapeutic properties and visual appeal by being directly infused into the soap batter or used as surface exfoliants. When added at specific times during the soap-making process, essential oils impart their fragrant overtones without exposure to high temperatures that might otherwise compromise their delicate smells.

It takes more skill than creating a pleasing scent to blend essential oils in aromatherapy-infused soaps. Apart from their scent, essential oils are selected for their medicinal properties. Formulations intended for skin prone to acne may contain tea tree oil, which is highly valued for its antimicrobial and antibacterial properties. Soaps used during seasonal changes benefit from the refreshing note added by eucalyptus oil, which is well-known for its respiratory properties. These soaps' blend of botanicals and essential oils produces a sensory experience that invites consumers to lose themselves in the healing embrace of nature, going beyond simple washing.

Additionally, the aesthetic dimension of the craft is enhanced by the visual appeal of soaps enriched with herbs and aromatherapy. Adding botanicals to the soap produces vivid colors and detailed designs that elevate each bar to the status of a miniature artwork. Calendula petals, lavender buds, or rosemary leaves turn from decorative accents to essential elements that enhance the overall experience of the soap. Soap producers frequently experiment with molds, swirls, and layering processes to produce aesthetically striking designs that evoke the splendor of the natural world.

Clay minerals are added to herbal-infused soaps to improve their skin-loving qualities and aesthetic attractiveness. Earthy tones and purifying properties of clays add to the soap's cleansing effectiveness. Clays are also known for their detoxifying and purifying properties. Formulations emphasizing a light washing experience can benefit from adding kaolin clay, which is soothing and suitable for sensitive skin. Because of its ability to absorb, bentonite clay is increasingly used in soaps intended for oily or acne-prone skin types. Clays enriches the overall sensory experience and pairs well with the herbal and aromatherapy ingredients, making each use a spa-like treat.

Apart from the plant-based components, natural exfoliants like oats, seeds, or crushed coffee are sometimes included in herbal-infused soaps. These components offer further skin-beneficial properties and add to the soap's aesthetic appeal. Because of their calming and anti-inflammatory qualities, oats provide a mild exfoliating action for sensitive skin. Poppy and chia seeds, for example, give a more vigorous exfoliation that encourages skin renewal and a more radiant complexion. These organic additions complement the holistic philosophy of herbal-infused soaps by appealing to the touch and visual senses.

Herbal and aromatherapy-infused soaps pay homage to the long-standing customs of both fields, but they also show a contemporary awareness of ethical behavior and sustainability. The ethical treatment of the communities engaged in their cultivation and harvesting is guaranteed by the fair-trade rules frequently followed in sourcing botanicals and essential oils. Furthermore, the decision to use sustainable palm oil—a contentious component in the soap industry—reflects a dedication to environmental responsibility. Producers of soap in this particular sector aim to provide skin-nourishing goods that positively impact the earth and its inhabitants.

Herbal and aromatherapy-infused soaps have the therapeutic ability to address specific skincare conditions in addition to their immediate sensory experience. Various advantages are provided by formulations enhanced with herbal substances recognized for their beneficial effects on the skin. Because of its relaxing and anti-inflammatory properties, chamomile is a main ingredient in soaps made for sensitive or inflamed skin. Rosehip oil, high in vitamins and antioxidants, is used in products that fight aging and promote skin renewal. By incorporating these botanical components, herbal-infused soaps become companions in the quest for healthy, glowing skin rather than just washing agents.

Furthermore, these soaps' incorporation of aromatherapy principles offers a doorway to emotional wellbeing. Bathing becomes a therapeutic practice because essential oils can affect mood and emotions. Due to its relaxing qualities, lavender essential oil is a salve for tension and anxiety, encouraging people to decompress. The bathing experience is infused with vitality and happiness by the uplifting scents of citrus oils. Herbal-infused soaps incorporating aromatherapy demonstrate a comprehensive approach to self-care that acknowledges the connection between mental and physical health.

Herbal and aromatherapy-infused soaps witness the durability of natural cures and the growing trend of incorporating sensory experiences into everyday routines in the soap-making industry. Herbalism and aromatherapy are becoming more popular, which aligns with a more significant cultural trend towards self-care, mindfulness, and getting back outside. Customers looking for products that go beyond the norm are drawn to these soaps' close relationship with the illustrious histories of herbal medicine and aromatic plant essences. The world of herbal and aromatherapy-infused soaps contains limitless possibilities for innovation, sensory enjoyment, and a return to the healing embrace of nature as soap manufacturers continue to explore the enormous palette of botanicals and essential oils.

CHAPTER VI

Packaging and Presentation

Sustainable And Eco-Friendly Packaging Options

The handmade soap industry is constantly changing and with it. Eco-friendly and sustainable methods are not limited to soap formulation; they also apply to the packaging in which these handcrafted products are packaged. In an effort to preserve the principles of ethical and responsible production, soap manufacturers are growing more interested in sustainable and eco-friendly packaging alternatives as public awareness of environmental issues and the ecological impact of consumer goods grows. Handmade soap packaging plays a vital role in the larger story of sustainability, tackling issues like resource depletion, waste production, and the industry's overall environmental impact.

Using simple, biodegradable materials is a popular option for sustainable soap packaging. Plastic or non-recyclable packaging is replaced by cardboard boxes or craft paper, frequently decorated with straightforward and environmentally friendly printing methods. Due to their natural decomposition, these materials have a less ecological impact and less long-term load on landfills. The trend toward more straightforward, more transparent packaging emphasizes the handmade and natural qualities of the soap it contains while also being in line with eco-conscious ideals.

Moreover, soap manufacturers looking into eco-friendly packaging solutions frequently choose recycled materials. Materials that would otherwise add to the environmental burden are given a second life through recycled paper, cardboard, and even post-consumer recycled plastic. This method reroutes trash back into the manufacturing cycle, addressing resource extraction and energy usage issues. Using recycled materials shows a dedication to the circular economy's guiding principles, which promote resource efficiency and waste reduction toto create a more regenerative and sustainable system.

Soap manufacturers who are dedicated to environmentally friendly packaging not only select sustainable materials but also frequently use cutting-edge design and packaging strategies that optimize effectiveness and reduce waste. Simple, effective designs that eliminate unnecessary embellishments or excess packaging not only minimize environmental impact but also enhance overall aesthetic appeal. In sustainable packaging, when the goal is to provide the product in a form that is both useful and environmentally responsible, the idea of "less is more" becomes a guiding principle.

Recyclable and biodegradable packaging materials are yet another important advancement in the soap industry's quest for sustainability. Compostable films, plant-based bioplastic, and even packaging created from agricultural waste are materials that provide an alternative to standard plastics that linger in the environment for a long time. These substances decompose organically and return to the planet without leaving a trace. The use of compostable and biodegradable packaging promotes a more regenerative relationship with the environment by being in line with the circularity of natural systems, where trash turns into a nutrient for the soil.

In a drastic divergence from standard packaging practices, soap manufacturers are also investigating the idea of "naked" or package-free soap choices. Soaps that are marketed without any exterior packaging, or "naked" soaps, help significantly reduce waste. This strategy encourages customers to adopt a more direct and tactile relationship with the soap and reevaluate the need for packaging. The idea of "naked soaps" appeals to people who are trying to live a zero-waste lifestyle and goes against the norm on how goods should be used and displayed.

Furthermore, manufacturers of soap that are dedicated to sustainable packaging frequently use careful labeling techniques. Using soy-based inks or other eco-friendly printing alternatives, minimalist and recyclable labels can create an eco-conscious and harmonious presentation. Labels that dissolve or dissolve in water are a creative solution that removes the need to take the labels off the packaging and dispose of them separately before recycling the packaging. The overarching objective of minimizing the environmental impact of a product's whole lifecycle, from production to disposal, aligns with these conscious labeling methods.

Another important factor in sustainable soap packaging is using reused or multipurpose containers. Glass jars, metal tins, and even reusable wooden containers are among the choices that soap manufacturers investigate. These containers' long lifespan beyond their first usage is made possible by their strength and visual appeal, which encourages users to incorporate them into their daily lives for various uses. Reusability encourages a more deliberate and thoughtful attitude to consumption while challenging the widespread culture of single-use packaging.

Soap makers frequently work with manufacturers and suppliers who share their dedication to environmentally friendly practices in their pursuit of sustainability. For a more comprehensive and responsible approach, forming alliances with businesses that place a high value on eco-certification adherence, ethical manufacturing practices, and sustainable procurement of packaging materials is recommended. Through these partnerships, it is ensured that all aspects of the soap-making process—from the final packaging to the raw materials—reflect a shared commitment to environmental care.

In addition, soap manufacturers consider the carbon footprint linked to the shipping and delivery of their goods. Reducing transportation-related emissions is facilitated by collaborating with neighboring suppliers and sourcing goods locally. In addition to being in line with ecological standards, the emphasis on patronizing local enterprises promotes community and camaraderie among those working in the soap sector. Several soap manufacturers also look into carbon offset schemes to lessen the harmful effects of transportation on the environment, indicating their continued dedication to ethical and environmentally responsible business practices.

Beyond individual actions, the soap-making community is adopting eco-friendly packaging solutions to support a more significant cultural movement towards sustainability. The community's exchange of information and experiences encourages teamwork and creativity, leading to investigating novel and long-lasting solutions. Social media groups, online forums, and soap-making gatherings provide venues for idea-sharing, problem-solving, and communal visioning of a more sustainable future for the art.

Furthermore, encouraging the use of ecological soap packaging requires vital consumer education. Soap manufacturers invest in open and honest communication regarding the packaging options they choose, offering details on the environmental factors that inform their decisions. Soap makers enable people to make informed and conscientious decisions by educating consumers about the environmental impact of packaging and providing eco-friendly alternatives. Transparent information exchange builds a community of environmentally concerned consumers and a sense of accountability.

In conclusion, the handmade soap industry's investigation of environmentally friendly and sustainable packaging solutions shows a dedication to ethical production practices and environmental care. Soap producers actively look for alternatives to traditional packaging materials and techniques because they are motivated by a shared ethos of conscious consumerism and ecological awareness. The soap industry is leading the way towards a more sustainable and regenerative approach, embracing minimalist designs and reused containers, as well as using biodegradable and compostable ingredients. With the increasing adoption of these measures, the handmade soap industry not only lessens its environmental impact but also acts as a model for other industries to adopt eco-friendly packaging and promote a sustainable culture.

Tips For Branding and Marketing Handmade Soaps

Efficient branding and marketing are essential to success in the ever-changing and cutthroat homemade soap crafting industry. Creating a brand that appeals to customers, connecting with their target market, and distinguishing out in a crowded market are obstacles artisan soap producers face, who are frequently passionate about what they do. Handmade soap branding and marketing is more than just coming up with a clever phrase or eye-catching logo; it also entails crafting a story that captures the brand's essence, forging a distinct identity, and carefully targeting potential consumers. To assist soap makers in creating a solid and enduring brand, this section delves into a wide range of branding and marketing strategies for handmade soaps. It does this by examining the nuances of consumer involvement, visual identity, internet presence, storytelling, and ethical considerations.

An engaging story faithful to the brand is essential for successful soap branding. To engage customers more deeply, the origin, inspiration, and artisan's journey of the soap become crucial components of the story. Makers of artisanal soap need to be genuine in their brand narrative so that consumers can develop an emotional bond with the product. The brand narrative is the cornerstone around which all other branding components are constructed, regardless of whether the soap is motivated by the creator's experiences, cultural influences, or dedication to sustainability. This story gives the soap a sense of genuineness, openness, and relatability, turning it from a commodity into a choice that customers find significant and unique.

The way a visual identity represents a business and shapes consumer perception of handmade soaps is crucial. Brand identification and recall are enhanced by visually appealing and consistent branding features, such as a unique logo, color scheme, and packaging design. The brand story, ethos, and values should be reflected in the visual identity. Soap manufacturers need to take the time to craft a visually appealing and unified presentation that will stick out on store shelves or online. As the initial point of contact for customers, the packaging design, in particular, should be aesthetically beautiful and communicate the soap's distinctive selling points, which could include its natural ingredients, sustainable production methods, or artisanal craftsmanship.

Handmade soap manufacturers must have a strong web presence to succeed in the digital age. The online shop is an exciting and user-friendly website that offers a way to showcase products, tell the brand's story, and process online payments. To increase visibility and expand their audience, soap manufacturers ought to optimize their websites for search engines (SEO). Enhancing the online purchasing experience with well-written product descriptions and excellent images gives potential customers confidence. Furthermore, using e-commerce features facilitates smooth transactions, broadening the brand's audience beyond regional marketplaces.

Social media platforms are practical tools that soap producers can use to engage with their audience, create a community, and present their products. Developing a solid social media strategy means choosing the proper channels for the target audience, publishing interesting information regularly, and encouraging deep connections with followers. With well-chosen photos and tales, visual media like Instagram work incredibly well for highlighting the artistic appeal of handcrafted soaps. Using social media to promote product releases, customer testimonials, and behind-the-scenes looks helps develop a brand narrative and a devoted supporters following.

Content marketing is a useful tactic for soap branding. It allows soap producers to disseminate information, analysis, and anecdotes about their art. The company can establish itself as an authority in the handmade soap sector by publishing blog entries, articles, or videos that highlight ingredients, explain the soap-making process, or provide skincare advice. In addition to increasing the brand's credibility, producing worthwhile and shareable content increases website traffic. It builds a feeling of community among clients passionate about handmade goods and natural treatments.

Partnerships and collaborations inside and outside the soap industry offer opportunities to connect and interact with a larger audience. Handmade soaps can reach new markets and demographics through cooperative ventures with other craftsmen, influencers, or complementary businesses. Joint product launches, collaborative events, or cross-promotions are examples of partnerships that foster a mutually beneficial connection for all parties. Finding authentic and relevant partnerships while also aligning with the brand's values and the target audience's needs is crucial.

Consumer interaction and feedback are crucial in determining how people view handmade soap companies. Establishing channels for consumer communication, such as surveys, social media polls, or feedback forms, invites users to contribute their thoughts, ideas, and experiences. Establishing a commitment to customer satisfaction and fostering trust can be achieved immediately and carefully responding to consumer requests and feedback. Positive customer reviews and testimonials can be displayed as reliable recommendations that influence potential customers on the brand's website and social media pages.

Creating a devoted consumer base within the brand experience takes exclusivity and uniqueness. Customizable packaging options, special discounts for repeat customers, and limited-edition releases can enhance a sense of appreciation and exclusivity. Manufacturers of soaps can use consumer data to develop focused advertising campaigns that provide individualized advice or first access to new goods. Brands may cultivate a sense of customer loyalty that extends beyond transactional relationships by providing them with a sense of worth and recognition.

Sustainable practices and ethical considerations are fundamental to modern consumer ideals, and soap manufacturers increasingly integrate ethical principles into their brands. Ethical factors enhance a brand's attractiveness and image, from using eco-friendly packaging to obtaining natural and cruelty-free products. Clear communication about certifications, ethical practices, and the brand's dedication to social and environmental responsibility builds consumer trust. It draws in a rising market of ethically conscious buyers looking for items that reflect their beliefs.

Adding storytelling components to product descriptions and promotional materials strengthens the business's and its customers' emotional bond while giving the brand more dimension. Soap producers can incorporate storytelling into their communication, describing the meaning behind each soap, the advantages of particular components, or the cultural significance of a specific formulation rather than just listing ingredients and attributes. With the help of this narrative approach, buying soap becomes an immersive experience that lets consumers relate to the product on an emotional and intimate level.

Engaging in pop-up events, craft fairs, or local markets gives soap producers a chance to interact directly with consumers, get feedback immediately, and highlight their goods' tactile and sensory qualities. Compared to internet purchases alone, in-person interactions allow clients to experience handcrafted soaps' quality, texture, and aroma, strengthening their bond. These events' personal touch and face-to-face connection promote brand loyalty and create enduring memories.

Maintaining relevance in the ever-evolving handmade soap market requires embracing innovation and keeping up with industry trends. Soap manufacturers should monitor changes in the market, consumer preferences, and emerging technology to modify their branding and marketing plans. Customers who are looking for novelty and creativity in their skincare regimens can be drawn to a brand that incorporates unique products, innovative formulations, or cutting-edge packaging.

In conclusion, a comprehensive strategy incorporating storytelling, visual identity, internet presence, consumer interaction, and ethical considerations is necessary to brand and market handcrafted soaps successfully.

Combining these components creates a brand that goes beyond the transactional aspect of business and develops an emotional bond with customers. In addition to helping soap producers stand out in a crowded market, authentic communication of the brand's story, values, and distinctive offerings fosters consumer loyalty and a sense of brand loyalty. The art of branding and marketing becomes a dynamic and ever-evolving adventure that propels artisanal soap manufacturers toward lasting success and recognition as the handmade soap industry continues to develop.

Creating An Appealing and Cohesive Product Line

A careful balance of strategic planning, creative thinking, and in-depth knowledge of market dynamics goes into creating a line of handcrafted, appealing, and well-coordinated soap. Passionate about what they do, handmade soap makers frequently set out to develop products that appeal to a broad spectrum of customers while showcasing their creative flare. Every facet of the product line, from choosing a theme and design style to guaranteeing product variety and consistency, adds to the overall brand identity and customer experience. This section delves into the essential factors and approaches to designing a visually appealing and well-coordinated handmade soap line. It provides information on themes, product differentiation, visual coherence, and the dynamic relationships among individual soaps in the more extensive collection.

Differentiation is the key to a successful range of handcrafted soap products. With the handmade soap market growing, it's becoming more important to separate from the competition to draw in and keep clients. Differentiation can take many forms, such as inventive soap shapes, specialist formulations for particular skin types, or unusual component combinations. To ascertain what areas their product line may excel in, soap producers must assess consumer preferences, market trends, and gaps in the competition. In addition to differentiating the brand, this distinction enables soap manufacturers to carve out a position in the highly competitive market.

Creating a unified product range that conveys a single brand identity heavily relies on visual uniformity. Ensuring a consistent visual theme throughout packaging design, soap forms, and colors improves brand recognition and promotes professionalism. A uniform color scheme, logo placement, and font selections enhance a visually coherent product line. Whether they want to communicate a bright and fun aesthetic, a minimalist and modern design, or a rustic, natural vibe, soap producers should consider the overall aesthetic appeal they want to portray. The brand's identity is further reinforced by maintaining consistency in product photography, ensuring that pictures from the product line have a comparable aesthetic.

A handcrafted soap product line gains depth and narrative from thematic cohesiveness. Individual soap operas are brought together by establishing a central idea or topic to produce a compelling plot that appeals to viewers. Seasons, nature, cultural influences, and even the soap maker's personal journey can inspire themes. For instance, a botanical-inspired product line can include a variety of soaps named after and infused with a distinct plant extract, resulting in a unified assortment that honors the diversity of nature. In addition to offering a framework for creativity, thematic coherence helps customers remember and interact with the product range.

For soap producers, developing a product line requires striking a careful balance between variety and cohesiveness. Variety in soap compositions, smells, and designs ensures that the product range stays dynamic and appealing to a broad audience while upholding a unified theme and visual consistency. Variety can include several soap bases to meet the demands of different skin types, such as olive oil, goat milk, or shea butter. Soap producers can cater to individual preferences by offering a choice of scents, from stimulating citrus to relaxing lavender. Furthermore, using various soap forms, textures, or design approaches gives the coherent product line a sense of surprise and exploration.

When designing a line of handcrafted soap products that appeal to customers, keeping the target market in mind is essential. Determining the target market's demographics, tastes, and way of life helps with judgments about soap formulas, fragrances, and overall branding. For example, a product line targeted at youthful, trend-focused people may emphasize bright colors and creative designs. At the same time, a brand for eco-conscious consumers might concentrate on sustainability in ingredients and packaging. When a product line is created to meet the particular requirements and tastes of the target market, its relevance and attraction are heightened.

A focal point that can anchor the brand identity is added when the idea of a trademark soap is expanded upon within the product line. As a flagship product, the trademark soap embodies the company's spirit and becomes a familiar image to customers. This soap can be distinguished from the rest of the brand by its distinctive ingredients, creative design features, or proprietary composition. The hallmark soap serves as a focal point for the brand narrative, enabling soap producers to emphasize the ideals, inspirations, and process of manufacture.

Customer engagement and discovery are encouraged by limited-edition releases and seasonal offerings, which bring excitement and a feeling of urgency to the product line. Limited edition products can build consumer anticipation by coinciding with holidays, special occasions, or thematic inspirations. Seasonal variations, such as soaps with a winter or summer theme, not only give the product line diversity but also cater to the shifting tastes and moods of customers all year long. Customers are prompted to investigate the entire product line and show interest in limited editions because of the perceived scarcity and exclusivity.

Maintaining product consistency in terms of quality, fragrance, and performance is imperative to uphold client trust and loyalty. Customers will always have a dependable and satisfying experience with each soap in the product range if consistent. Soap makers ought to make an effort to consistently produce soap that meets the expected advantages without sacrificing quality from batch to batch. Customers can identify a specific fragrance with a company when there is consistency in the aroma, which helps with brand identification and recall. Overall, line consistency is influenced by quality control procedures, standardization of formulas, and product testing.

Analyzing production costs, market trends, and perceived value is necessary for strategic pricing within the product line. Soap manufacturers need to set prices commensurate with the caliber of their ingredients, their level of skill, and the distinctiveness of their handmade products. Different soaps in the product line may have varying prices depending on things like premium ingredients, intricate designs, or unique formulations. By providing a range of pricing points, the product line becomes more accessible to a broader audience by accommodating a variety of consumer budgets and preferences.

It is necessary to actively seek out and incorporate client feedback into the evolution of the product line to adopt a customer-centric approach. Insights, inclinations, and customer recommendations offer soap manufacturers insightful direction when they want to improve current products or launch new ones. There are various ways to get feedback and learn about client preferences, including social media platforms, customer surveys, and in-person contact at events or markets. Soap manufacturers strengthen their ties and improve their product lines by listening to their customers and improving based on their needs and preferences.

The lifespan of each soap in the product line must be considered for efficient inventory control and product rotation. While some soaps could be limited-edition, seasonal products with a brief shelf life, others might be long-term favorites. By monitoring inventory turnover and sales patterns, soap manufacturers can make well-informed judgments regarding which soaps to continue, retire, or reintroduce based on consumer demand. This strategy avoids stagnation and maximizes sales by keeping the product line flexible and adaptable to changing market conditions.

An array of handcrafted soap products' overall appeal is greatly influenced by their packaging design. Packaging that is visually appealing and consistent strengthens the brand's identity and influences consumer choices. The packaging should reflect the brand's beliefs and the sensory experience that the soap offers while also fitting well with the general theme and design of the product range. Furthermore, exciting and educational packaging can tell the tale of each soap, highlight its main components, and provide usage guidelines. This generally improves the consumer experience and forges a bond between the buyer and the product.

Using strategic marketing and promotion techniques is essential to getting the target market to know about the handmade soap product line. Email marketing, social media platforms, and partnerships with bloggers or influencers are ways to raise awareness and spark interest. All marketing collateral, including striking images and captivating product descriptions, should complement the line's overarching visual theme and story. Soap manufacturers can communicate with potential customers and highlight the distinctiveness of their product line through interactive campaigns, launch events, and online promotions.

In conclusion, striking a careful balance between distinction, visual consistency, thematic cohesiveness, and strategic variety is necessary to create an appealing and unified line of handcrafted soap products. To create a collection that embodies their creative vision and appeals to a wide range of consumers, soap makers must negotiate the complexity of consumer preferences, market dynamics, and brand identification. Soap producers can create a product line that stands out in the competitive market, encourages consumer loyalty, and captures the soul of their brand by embracing differentiation, upholding visual and thematic continuity, providing strategic diversity, and considering the target audience. Developing a fascinating product line is still a dynamic, iterative process that combines creativity, market awareness, and a strong love for the craft as the handmade soap industry grows.

CHAPTER VII

Troubleshooting and Quality Control

Common Issues in Soap Making and How to Address Them

Even though it's a creative and fulfilling activity, manufacturing soap might present some difficulties. Craftspeople producing handmade soap frequently encounter similar problems that affect every process step, from formulation to curing. Comprehending these obstacles and figuring out how to overcome them is essential to constantly making handcrafted soaps of superior quality. This thorough investigation addresses topics like choosing ingredients, formulating soap, pouring and tracing, curing, and resolving typical complications that may come up while manufacturing soap.

Deciding which ingredients to use is one of the most complex parts of producing soap. The classic method of making soap involves reacting oils and fats with sodium hydroxide, or lye, in a process known as saponification. However, the qualities of the soap can be significantly affected by the choice of oils and fats. Soap producers can customize their compositions using various oils to suit particular skin types and desired attributes. Common oils like palm, coconut, and olive add many aspects to the soap, including moisturizing, lathering, and hardness. However, selecting oils without knowing each one's unique qualities can result in an uneven finished product. For instance, a soap that is overly drying for the skin could be produced by using too much coconut oil. To solve this problem, soap producers should educate themselves on the characteristics of different oils and develop formulations that balance well for the soap's intended use.

Ingredient selection is strongly related to soap formulation, which is an essential phase in the soap-making process. A well-balanced formula is necessary to provide soap properties such as hardness, cleaning power, and lather. Making soap, meanwhile, may be difficult, particularly for first-timers. Too soft, too harsh, or prone to quick trace (the point when the soap batter thickens) are common problems. Online soap calculators are helpful for soap producers to solve formulation problems. They can assist in figuring out how much lye and water are appropriate for a specific blend of oils. These calculators allow for modifications before the soap-making process by offering insights into the expected qualities of the soap. Soap producers can improve their recipes by experimenting with tiny batches and meticulously documenting everything.

For soap manufacturers, the process of "trace and pour," which occurs when the soap batter achieves the proper consistency for molding, can be frustrating. Achieving the right trace is crucial for the appropriate formation of soap. However, the oils used and the method utilized (cold process, hot process, or melt and pour) can affect how quickly the trace occurs. Working with the soap batter can be problematic due to rapid trace, which can cause issues with pouring or molding. Conversely, sluggish traces could produce a soap that sets more slowly, impacting the finished texture. Soap producers should modify their mixing methods and work at a pace that aligns with the particular needs of their recipe to address trace-related concerns. Adding components that slow down the saponification process, like a more significant proportion of olive oil, can be helpful for people who are suffering fast trace.

A critical but frequently disregarded step in the soap-making process is curing. Curing produces a softer and more durable soap by allowing the soap to solidify and complete its chemical reactions. Nevertheless, impatience may cause one to apply soap before completely drying, making the experience less enjoyable and less effective. Uneven hardness, discoloration, or a persistent lye smell are common problems throughout the curing process. To alleviate these worries, soap makers should follow the advised curing times, varying from a few weeks to several months, depending on the soap formula. Uneven hardness can be avoided with proper storage practices, such as enabling air to circulate the curing bars. Supplementing the mixture with antioxidants such as vitamin E will help minimize discoloration, and adding essential oils or aroma oils can help cover up any lingering lye smell.

All soap-making processes require troubleshooting, and different issues may come up along the way. One frequent problem that detracts from the finished soap's appearance is the existence of air bubbles. To solve this issue, which frequently arises during the pouring stage, soap makers should gently tap the mold on a flat surface or release trapped air with a skewer. Soda ash, a powdery white residue that can accumulate on the soap's surface during curing and detract from its look, presents another difficulty. Soap producers might use rubbing alcohol spray or cover the soap with plastic wrap immediately after putting it into the mold to avoid soda ash. Furthermore, fading or morphing of color can happen, particularly when natural colorants are used. To solve this problem, soap manufacturers can use a variety of colorants, use additions like kaolin clay to stabilize hues, or accept any inevitable natural fluctuations.

Fragrance retention problems can also arise for soap producers, causing the scent to fade or alter over time. This can be addressed by experimenting with different fragrance concentrations, utilizing fragrance oils specially designed for soap-making, and ensuring that the fragrance is incorporated adequately throughout the process. Furthermore, temperature changes during saponification may result in glycerine rivers, where the soap forms transparent streaks or rivers. Soap producers can consider insulating the mold or lowering the temperature of the oils and lye solution before mixing to address glycerine rivers.

Soap makers can need help with the texture of their products, such as crumbly or mushy consistency. Errors in ingredient measurements or concerns with the saponification process frequently cause these problems. Soap producers should meticulously follow their soap recipe, ensuring precise amounts and thorough mixing to address texture-related issues. The final texture can also be affected by varying the formulation's hard-to-soft oil ratio. Furthermore, using soap that contains a lot of lye, which indicates that the soap has not fully saponified and could be harmful to the skin, can be very concerning. Soap producers should ensure their measurements are correct, get a reliable scale, and follow safety guidelines while handling lye to solve this. There may be difficulties unique to the kind of soap that soap producers are producing. Achieving the desired design in the complex art of swirls and patterns can be challenging. Problems could include inconsistent color blending or an unintended appearance of the swirl pattern. Soap makers should experiment with various pouring techniques, work quickly but carefully to create intricate patterns, and monitor the viscosity of the soap batter during the pour to overcome these problems. Additionally, issues with the formulation's fitness for the intended function may arise for soap makers creating specialty soaps, like shampoo bars or razor soaps. To overcome these obstacles, it is necessary to investigate each kind of soap's particular needs, consider variables such as shaving preferences or hair type, and add ingredients that meet those criteria.

In conclusion, solving typical soap-making problems requires a blend of expertise, experience, and flexibility. Soap makers should approach every step of the process with a thorough perspective, learning as much as they can about the nuances of the craft, from choosing ingredients to curing. Learning is aided by using tools like internet calculators, small-batch experimentation, and recording every soap-making session. Whether the issue is with texture, smell, or look, troubleshooting requires a thorough approach and a desire to improve skills gradually. Making handcrafted soaps that are fulfilling, distinctive, and of high quality requires soap makers to negotiate the complexities of their trade, and dealing with frequent problems becomes an essential part of that journey.

Ensuring Consistency and Quality in Your Soap Products

For handcrafted soap producers, maintaining consistency and quality in handmade soap products is crucial since it demonstrates their devotion to their craft and provides clients with a dependable and pleasurable experience. Every step of the soap-making process, from ingredient selection and formulation to production methods, curing, and final presentation, requires a multidimensional strategy to achieve this uniformity and quality. This thorough investigation explores the essential factors and techniques soap manufacturers can use to maintain excellent standards in their handmade soap products, encouraging client happiness, repeat business, and a favorable reputation among the ever-expanding artisanal soap aficionados.

The meticulous selection of ingredients is the cornerstone of handmade soap's consistency and excellence. Every element, including oils, fats, perfumes, and colorants, gives the finished product unique qualities. Premium, ethically sourced ingredients must be a top priority for soap manufacturers to maintain a uniform standard throughout their product range. This entails investigating potential suppliers, learning about raw materials' provenance and manufacturing processes, and looking for reliable vendors with a reputation for excellence. A soap manufacturer can create soaps that meet and surpass client expectations by starting with high-quality ingredients.

Soap makers use their imagination and experience to create a well-balanced and efficient soap recipe at the crucial formulation stage. A dedication to testing and refining, exact measurements, and a thorough understanding of each ingredient's characteristics are necessary to achieve consistency in soap formulas. To keep consistency in the soap-making process, soap calculators—which help determine the right amounts of lye and water for a particular mix of oils—become indispensable resources. To continuously enhance and perfect their recipes, soap makers must also maintain thorough records of their compositions, noting modifications and alterations. By taking such care, every batch of soap is guaranteed to have the desired properties and attributes, giving consumers a dependable and consistent product.

Issues with consistency and quality of the finished soap can arise from the obstacles presented by the soap-making process itself. For correct molding to occur and for the soap to reach the required texture and look, it is necessary to achieve a uniform trace, or the point at which the soap batter thickens. For a given soap recipe, stick blending, hand stirring, or mixing the two are essential for the proper trace. Maintaining consistency in mixing techniques and being conscious of the distinct qualities of various oils help ensure a consistent result with every batch. Furthermore, to preserve quality and consistency during the trace, it is necessary to apply the proper corrective measures and have a thorough grasp of the soap-making process to address potential problems like air bubbles or quick thickening.

Curing—a sometimes disregarded step in the soap-making process—is essential to ensure the lifespan and quality of handcrafted soap products. Curing completes saponification and ensures the soap is safe, gentle, and long-lasting. It also allows the soap to harden. Curing periods must remain constant for the entire product line to stay consistent. Soap producers must follow prescribed curing times, which might vary based on the soap formulation and can be anywhere from a few weeks to many months. A consistent and superior final product results from proper curing conditions, including sufficient air circulation around the curing bars and curing racks to prevent uneven hardness.

Soap producers have to deal with scent retention issues to maintain consistency and high quality. A crucial component of many handmade soaps is fragrance, which gives consumers a pleasant and fragrant experience. However, maintaining a solid aroma for the duration of the soap's shelf life can be a challenging undertaking. Essential techniques include experimenting with different concentrations, using fragrance oils created explicitly for soap-making, and adding smells at the right point. Handmade soap producers can improve their soaps' quality and attractiveness by carefully considering their formulas' fragrance components and providing a consistent olfactory experience for their customers.

Problems with texture, such as crumbly or too-soft soap, can affect how a product feels and are frequently connected to methods used in formulation and mixing.

Carefully following their recipes will ensure precise proportions and a well-balanced combination of hard and soft oils for soap producers. The desired texture can be achieved consistently by experimenting with different combinations and adjusting the ratio of oils in the mixture. The difficulties associated with texture also emphasize how crucial it is to spend money on precise scales, adhere to established practices, and conduct exhaustive testing to resolve any possible problems before the finished product is delivered to clients.

Ensuring the safety and quality of handcrafted soap products requires addressing the possibility of lye-heavy soap. Lye is an essential ingredient in creating soap, but it must be utilized carefully to prevent using too much in the finished product. When using lye, soap producers should carefully verify their measurements, purchase precise scales, and follow safety instructions. Maintaining a consistent focus on safety procedures enhances the soap's quality and builds a credible and accountable brand image.

Producers of specialty soaps, like shampoo bars or shave soaps, face particular difficulties because of the demands placed on these goods. Extensive investigation into the needs of every kind of soap is necessary to guarantee that compositions serve the desired function. When creating custom soaps, variables must be considered, including skin sensitivity, shaving preferences, and hair type. Soap makers can consistently deliver superior specialty goods by customizing ingredients and procedures to satisfy individual needs.

Another essential factor in guaranteeing the overall quality of handcrafted soap products is consistency in appearance. Consumers frequently associate a brand's aesthetic appeal with it. Thus, soap manufacturers must work to live up to these expectations constantly. For consistent and visually beautiful outcomes, techniques like color integration, swirls, and patterns must be used accurately and skillfully. To achieve consistent and aesthetically pleasing designs, soap makers should experiment with different pouring techniques, work steadily, and pay attention to the viscosity of the soap batter during the pour.

Solving typical problems that may arise in handmade soap settings becomes essential to preserving consistency and quality. For example, if air bubbles are present, you can remove trapped air during the pouring step by using a skewer or gently striking the mold on a flat surface. Soap makers have two options for preventing soda ash, a white powder that can appear on the soap's surface while curing: they can cover the soap with plastic wrap right away after pouring it or give it a ring spray. Color-related problems, including color fading or morphing, can also be troubleshooted by soap producers. They can try new colorants, use additions like kaolin clay to stabilize colors, or accept any inevitable natural fluctuations in color.

One often-overlooked way to guarantee the overall quality of handcrafted soap goods is through consistent pricing procedures. For the soap to remain distinctive and for the business to be sustainable, the price structure must consider the high caliber of the ingredients, the craftsmanship, and the product's unique features. When setting their prices, soap manufacturers should consider the competitive environment, market trends, and production costs. Soap manufacturers may accommodate a wide range of consumer budgets while upholding a quality standard across their product line by providing a range of price points.

It is essential to take a customer-centric approach to guarantee consistency and quality in handcrafted soap products. Actively seeking and utilizing client feedback can provide significant insights into customer preferences, concerns, and expectations during the soap-making process. Feedback can be gathered through social media, customer surveys, and face-to-face interactions at events or fairs. Soap manufacturers strengthen their relationships with customers and improve their products by listening to their feedback and improving based on client demands and preferences.

A final layer of consistency in branding and presentation enhances handmade soap products' overall quality. Creating a consistent brand identity through visual components, including packaging, marketing materials, and logos, enhances a professional and reliable image. Optical coherence also applies to product photography, guaranteeing that pictures from one product line to the next have the same aesthetic and caliber. A brand's emotional connection to its customers is strengthened when its values, mission, and captivating brand story are incorporated into marketing materials. This reinforces the perception of quality and dependability.

To sum up, guaranteeing consistency and quality in handcrafted soap products is a dynamic and complex undertaking that calls for meticulous attention to detail, a dedication to perfection, and an ongoing quest for development. Every step of the soap-making process, from formulating and choosing ingredients to production methods, curing, and consumer interaction, is vital to maintaining high standards. Through a systematic approach, experience-based learning, and constant attention to customer feedback, soap makers can surpass expectations and become recognized as suppliers of superior handmade soap products in the artisanal soap industry and elsewhere.

Quality Testing Methods

Ensuring that handcrafted soaps fulfill the highest standards of excellence and safety, quality testing procedures are essential to soap-making. To provide consumers with a dependable and consistent experience, artisans are using rigorous testing processes to make unique and practical items. This thorough investigation explores the several quality testing techniques used in soap production, including component evaluation, formulation testing, trace evaluation, curing analysis, and final product inspection. Soap manufacturers can improve the overall quality of their handmade soaps, gaining clients' trust and building a reputation for excellence within the artisanal soap community by incorporating these testing procedures into their craft.

A careful evaluation of ingredients is the first step on the path to high-quality soap-making. Before adding oils, fats, lye, and other ingredients to the soap recipe, craftspeople should carefully inspect each one to ensure it is pure and high-quality. This includes investigating potential suppliers, checking compliance with industry standards, and vetting the sourcing procedures. While lye should be examined for purity and granular form, oils may be evaluated based on color, consistency, and odor. Common additions to handmade soaps, fragrances, and colorants are also examined for quality, stability, and appropriateness for the intended use. Thorough ingredient testing lays the groundwork for a high-quality soap by averting possible problems that inferior or tainted ingredients might bring about.

A crucial step in the soap-making process is formulation testing, which entails exact measurements, meticulous computations, and online soap calculators to establish the right lye and water ratios for a particular oil combination. Testing the quality of the soap's formulation guarantees that it has the right amount of hardness, cleansing power, lather, and moisturizing qualities. Before scaling up to more considerable production levels, soap makers should do small-scale tests or pilot batches to assess the formulation's performance and make necessary improvements. The artisans who focus on the formulation testing process can improve their recipes, spot possible problems, and set a uniform benchmark for their handmade soaps.

Determining when the soap batter reaches the ideal thickness for pouring or molding is a crucial step in the soap-making process: trace examination. A consistent trace must be obtained for the soap to have the desired texture and look. This step uses various testing techniques to evaluate the trace, such as measuring the thickness with stick blenders, spoon tests, and the consistency of the batter. Trace speed is affected by the type of oil used and the particular method of creating soap (cold process, hot process, or melt and pour). Therefore, soap producers must modify their methods accordingly. Preserving the appropriate texture in each batch of soap by means of regular trace testing improves the final product's overall quality and look.

Curing analysis is a crucial way of quality control that concentrates on the soap-making process after manufacturing. Curing completes the saponification process and ensures a softer, more durable soap by allowing the soap to solidify. Determining the proper curing period for each soap recipe—which can vary from a few weeks to several months—is the first step in testing the curing process. During the curing process, producers should periodically check their soap to ensure it achieves the proper hardness and doesn't develop problems like uneven curing or discoloration. A consistent and superior final product results from proper curing conditions, which include using curing racks and allowing enough air to circulate the curing bars.

Final product inspection is performed as a last resort for guaranteeing the general quality of handcrafted soap. This extensive testing entails closely inspecting the completed soap bars' sensory and visual attributes. Visual inspection involves evaluating each soap's color, texture, and design components to ensure it meets the intended standards. Testing the scent, lather, and general feel of the soap while it's being used is known as sensory evaluation. To obtain a variety of viewpoints, soap manufacturers should perform their sensory testing and consult with dependable testers or focus groups. The final product inspection is a thorough evaluation that enables artisans to see any variations from the target quality and make the required corrections for subsequent production runs.

Soap producers may use specialized tests in addition to these basic testing techniques to evaluate particular characteristics of their handmade soaps. For example, pH testing determines the soap's acidity or alkalinity and confirms that it is within a safe and appropriate range for application on the skin. Elevated pH values may yield abrasive and desiccating soaps, whereas abnormally low pH values can suggest insufficient saponification, which could result in heavy lye bars. Testing the soap's pH offers essential information about its composition and possible effects on skin health.

Soap manufacturers also use specialist techniques like microbial testing to ensure the final product does not contain dangerous germs. Since the saponification process gives soap its inherent antibacterial qualities, more research might be done, particularly if other components present, including botanical additions, raise concerns about microbes. For the health and satisfaction of customers, handmade soaps must be guaranteed to be microbiologically safe.

Soap manufacturers may also investigate the use of sophisticated analytical methods, such as mass spectrometry or gas chromatography, to thoroughly examine the soap's chemical makeup to improve quality testing. Fatty acids, essential oils, and additives are just a few components whose existence and concentration can be understood using these techniques. While some artisanal soap makers with access to the necessary equipment may use these sophisticated procedures for a more thorough quality assessment, they may be more popular in commercial soap manufacture.

In addition to spotting possible problems, quality testing techniques promote innovation and ongoing soap production development. To find areas for improvement, soap manufacturers can test several formulas, ingredients, or processing methods side by side. Using an iterative testing process, soap formulas are improved and evolved, enabling craftspeople to keep up with market trends, consumer preferences, and technological improvements.

Following best practices for safety and hygiene goes hand in hand with embracing a commitment to quality testing. Routine equipment calibration, adherence to established protocols, and the use of protective gear during the soap-making process facilitate a safe and regulated environment. Incorporating safety procedures into their testing procedures allows soap manufacturers to promote a responsible and professional image among the artisanal soap community while also attending to the health and welfare of their consumers.

To sum up, quality testing techniques are essential resources for soap producers committed to creating outstanding handcrafted soaps. Every procedure is vital to guaranteeing uniformity, security, and overall quality, from component evaluation to formulation testing, trace assessment, curing analysis, final product inspection, and specialized testing. Prioritizing thorough testing helps soap producers fulfill the high standards of their clients and advance the standing and expansion of the handmade soap industry. A dedication to detailed and cutting-edge testing procedures remains a pillar for artisans hoping to distinguish in this vibrant and creative sector as the demand for distinctive and premium handmade soaps keeps growing.

CHAPTER VIII

The Business of Handmade Soap

Starting A Small-Scale Soap-Making Business

Launching a small-scale soap manufacturing company allows entrepreneurs to blend entrepreneurship, creativity, and skill in a growing market. Due to consumer preferences for natural, distinctive, and locally created goods, the soap industry has seen a rise in demand for handcrafted, artisanal soaps. This thorough book covers all the essential factors, procedures, and tactics to consider when starting a small-scale soap manufacturing company. It covers topics like market analysis, business planning, legal compliance, setting up production, marketing, and continuing management. Aspiring soap manufacturers can turn their passion into a profitable, long-lasting commercial endeavor by identifying five essential elements.

Market research is the first and most crucial step in starting a profitable soap company. Finding the USP—unique selling proposition—that makes the company stand out requires understanding the target market, consumer preferences, and market trends. In-depth market research entails examining the tastes, buying patterns, and demographics of consumers with handcrafted soaps. Exploring virtual and physical rivals offers perceptions into current gaps in the industry and chances to stand out. Crucial choices like the kinds of soaps to sell, pricing schemes, and marketing tactics catered to the particular requirements and preferences of the target market are all influenced by the results of this research phase.

Creating a solid business plan is the next stage in launching a small-scale soap manufacturing company after gaining insightful industry knowledge. The business plan outlines the venture's vision, objective, goals, and operational strategies and acts as a road map. A thorough explanation of the soap goods, a target market study, a competitive landscape evaluation, financial predictions, and an extensive marketing strategy are all essential parts of the business plan. Initial costs, continuing operating costs, and revenue expectations should all be included in financial projections. In addition to acting as a roadmap for the entrepreneur, a well-written business plan is an essential tool for obtaining capital, alliances, or stakeholder support.

Opening a small-scale soap manufacturing company requires successfully navigating the regulatory environment. The legality and safety of the items are guaranteed by adherence to local, state, and federal regulations. Soap manufacturers should investigate and follow laws about cosmetics labeling, ingredient disclosure, and Good Manufacturing Practices (GMP). Comprehending the legal mandates for product testing, safety evaluations, and ingredient records enhances the overall credibility of the enterprise. Furthermore, securing the required licenses and permits—such as a company license and permissions from the health department—is essential to guaranteeing a legal and efficient operation.

Setting up the production area is an essential first step in starting a small-scale soap manufacturing company. The production area should have all the equipment and instruments required to make soap, such as molds, mixing tools, stainless steel pots, and safety gear. To comply with regulations and guarantee product quality, soap manufacturers should prioritize hygiene and cleanliness in their production area. Productivity and uniformity are enhanced by efficiently planning every step of the production process, from ingredient preparation to packaging. To satisfy rising demand, scalability in production capacity and process becomes crucial as the business expands.

Getting premium ingredients is essential to producing soap on a modest scale. Building connections with trustworthy suppliers of lye, oils, fats, colorants, and perfumes guarantees a steady and dependable supply chain. Soap producers should give preference to suppliers who use responsibly sourced ingredients in order to satisfy the increasing request from consumers for products that are socially and environmentally diligent. Undertaking comprehensive investigation on the ingredients' quality, provenance, and certifications enhances the handmade soaps' overall appeal and marketability. Establishing solid bonds with suppliers promotes dependability and trust, both of which are essential for the company's long-term prosperity.

Handmade soaps' branding and packaging are crucial in drawing in customers and developing a recognizable brand identity. Creating a logo that stands out, selecting a unified visual style, and creating a unique brand narrative all help create a brand that appeals to the intended market. Not only should packaging be eye-catching, but it should also be valuable and eco-friendly. Taking into account eco-friendly packaging alternatives is in line with customer desires. Regulation-compliant labeling must provide precise information on ingredients, usage guidelines, and safety measures. A well-crafted and visually appealing brand image raises the handmade soaps' perceived value overall, increasing their market competitiveness.

Building recognition and increasing sales for a small-scale soap manufacturing company requires marketing, which is dynamic and essential. A dedicated website or e-commerce platform must be used to establish an online presence to develop a multifaceted marketing plan. Soap makers can interact with potential clients and visually promote their products using social media platforms like Facebook, Pinterest, and Instagram. The company becomes recognized as an expert in its field by using content marketing, such as blogs and how-to guides for creating soap. Reaching a wider audience can also be accomplished via participating in local markets, craft fairs, or partnerships with nearby retailers. By practicing search engine optimization (SEO) techniques, a business can increase its online visibility and draw in potential clients looking for handcrafted soaps.

A small-scale soap manufacturer's capacity to maintain a profitable operation depends on its ability to set prices that work. Production costs, such as labor, raw materials, packaging, and overhead, should be considered when setting prices. Profitability depends on determining a reasonable and competitive retail price that covers costs and conforms to market expectations. Soap manufacturers can accommodate a variety of customer budgets by providing a range of price points. Certain items might justify their premium pricing by including value-added features like eco-friendly packaging, unusual formulas, or customisable options. Maintaining competitiveness and financial viability requires routinely analyzing and modifying pricing strategies in response to market developments, production costs, and competition pricing.

If small-scale soap makers want to reach a wider audience and increase sales, they must have a strong internet presence. Establishing a polished and easy-to-use website is a focal location for product displays, brand storytelling, and online transaction processing. Putting in place safe and smooth e-commerce features makes it simple for clients to look through, choose, and buy handcrafted soaps. Search engine optimization increases the website's exposure and generates natural traffic. Reaching a wider audience can also be accomplished by using online marketplaces like Etsy or Amazon Handmade. Building a steady and exciting social media presence enhances the online approach by encouraging community involvement and patronage.

A small-scale soap manufacturer's ability to develop and succeed depends heavily on its ability to engage and hear from its customers. Soap producers can engage with their audience by establishing clear communication channels like social media, email newsletters, and a responsive customer service system. Encouragement of client testimonials and reviews provide perceptions of the items' perceived worth and level of satisfaction. Positive brand perception is bolstered by immediately answering consumer questions, attending to issues, and considering constructive criticism. Creating an unforgettable and pleasurable shopping experience, providing discounts or loyalty plans, and continuously providing high-quality products are all necessary to cultivate a devoted clientele.

Strategic planning and thorough analysis of growth opportunities are necessary when scaling a small-scale soap manufacturing company. Scalable expansion is facilitated by evaluating consumer demand, diversifying product offers, and investigating new avenues for distribution. Enhancing awareness and reach can be achieved through collaborating with other artists or businesses for co-branded products or partnerships.

Putting money into marketing campaigns, including influencer partnerships or focused advertising, can draw in more clients. Scaling production requires careful planning to maintain consistent product quality, effective workflows, and the capacity to fulfill growing demand without sacrificing the handmade and artisanal features of the business.

A small soap production company needs to be managed and adjusted continuously to be successful in the long run. The business remains flexible and adaptable to changes in the market by routinely assessing and revising the financial predictions, marketing tactics, and business plans. Soap makers can proactively modify their offers and methods by remaining updated about consumer preferences, market developments, and regulatory revisions. The development of skills and ongoing education in marketing, business administration, and soapmaking all support the expansion and innovation of the company. Developing a robust and flexible mindset puts the company in a position to take advantage of new opportunities and overcome obstacles in the fast-paced soap market.

Launching a small-scale soap manufacturing company is an exciting adventure that blends creativity and business. Aspiring soap makers can turn their passion into a successful and long-lasting business endeavor by conducting in-depth market research, creating a detailed business plan, ensuring regulatory compliance, setting up efficient production processes, and implementing effective marketing strategies. The long-term growth and success of the company are primarily dependent on developing a solid brand, interacting with customers, and adjusting to the market. Small-scale soap producers are vital to the supply chain because of the growing desire for artisanal and handmade goods. These products offer distinctive, premium options to consumers seeking a conscientious and personalized skincare solution.

Legal Considerations and Regulations

Navigating the legal environment is vital to starting and running a soap manufacturing company. The safety, legality, and caliber of soap makers' goods are contingent upon their compliance with many rules, regardless of whether they produce handmade soaps from a home studio or expand production in a dedicated facility. This in-depth analysis explores the legal issues and regulations controlling the soap industry, including labeling specifications, product safety requirements, Good Manufacturing Practices (GMP), intellectual property protection, and local, state, and federal regulatory compliance. Recognizing and adhering to these legal issues helps maintain the integrity of the industry as a whole and protects the soap maker's business and consumer confidence.

Product labeling is one of the leading legal issues in the soap manufacturing sector. In addition to being required by law, precise and clear labeling is essential for building customer trust and openness. Manufacturers of soap are needed to abide by labeling regulations, such as those set forth by the US Food and Drug Administration (FDA). The product name, ingredient list, net weight, manufacturer's contact details, and usage guidelines should all be included on labels. By guaranteeing that customers have access to essential information regarding the soap's composition and usage, compliance with these labeling requirements promotes informed consumer decision-making and ensures product safety.

Soap makers have additional laws to follow regarding ingredient disclosure and general labeling requirements. The FDA requires that all ingredients in cosmetics, including soap, be listed in descending order of predominance on the product label. Each ingredient's common or normal name should be stated, and it is advised to utilize the INCI (International Nomenclature of Cosmetic Ingredients) designations. In addition to meeting legal requirements, this openness empowers customers—including those with allergies or sensitivities—to make knowledgeable decisions about the goods they apply to their skin.

Soap manufacturers must follow laws about product safety standards and disclose ingredients. While soap is generally considered safe when used according to directions, some formulas or additions may cause safety issues. For instance, soap manufacturers must ensure that all color additives used in cosmetics comply with FDA regulations or that they risk facing legal repercussions. Ensuring that soap products are free of dangerous ingredients, comply with microbiological safety standards, and undergo the required testing is vital for regulatory compliance and overall consumer safety.

A collection of regulations known as Good Manufacturing Practices (GMP) specify the procedures and settings in which soap and other cosmetics must be made to guarantee their high quality and safety. Although the FDA does not explicitly require GMP for soap manufacturers, following these guidelines is highly recommended. Keeping hygienic surroundings, appropriate tools, and precise record-keeping throughout the soap-making process are all part of adhering to GMP guidelines. This dedication to GMP reduces the possibility of contamination and ensures that the finished product is safe for consumer use and in line with industry best practices.

If soap makers develop original recipes, brands, or designs, protecting their intellectual property is an essential legal matter. Simple soap formulas might not be eligible for patent protection, but trademark protection might be available for branding components such as product names, logos, and eye-catching packaging. By providing legal protections against unapproved use by rivals, trademark registration with the relevant intellectual property offices aids in establishing and maintaining soap makers' brand identities. Non-disclosure agreements with suppliers, partners, and employees can also be used to preserve trade secrets, including unique formulas or processing techniques, keeping the private facets of the soap industry.

Soap manufacturers must adhere to all applicable local, state, and federal requirements to operate lawfully and responsibly. Home-based soap makers are frequently subject to local health department regulations, which establish labeling, hygiene, and production requirements. Jurisdiction laws can differ, so soap manufacturers should be aware of any unique rules that apply to cosmetics in their jurisdiction. Federal regulation of cosmetics is under the purview of the FDA. While soap is not classified as a cosmetic, some ingredients or statements on soap products could make them vulnerable to FDA examination. Comprehending and complying with these regulatory layers guarantees that soap manufacturers function within legal boundaries, cultivating a reliable and conscientious enterprise.

Regulations and environmental factors, particularly those about waste management and sustainable practices, are also relevant to the soap sector. Soap manufacturers need to be aware of local environmental laws that control how production wastes, like leftover soap batter or cleaning supplies, are disposed of. Implementing eco-friendly products, including using sustainable materials and biodegradable packaging, fits with consumer demands for items that are more ecologically sensitive and could improve brand reputation.

Product liability rules must be followed for soap makers to be legally protected. Even while handcrafted soaps are generally considered safe, unanticipated problems like allergic reactions or other adverse effects could occur. Sufficient liability insurance offers monetary defense against lawsuits about product safety. Soap manufacturers should speak with insurance experts to choose the right coverage for their particular business model. They should consider the goods' overall risk profile, distribution routes, and production scale.

Making soap involves navigating a sometimes-complicated legal environment, so it's essential to keep up with industry developments, legislative changes, and best practices. For soap makers looking for legal advice, trade associations, industry forums, and attorneys focusing on cosmetics or small enterprises can be invaluable resources. Participating in pertinent events and workshops and interacting with the soap-making community offers chances to exchange experiences, pick up tips from colleagues, and keep up with industry advancements.

Legal issues and regulations are crucial in the soap sector, influencing how soap producers create, manufacture, label, and sell their goods. Dealing with the legal system is a complex process that involves many different aspects, such as preserving intellectual property, following local, state, and federal rules, and complying to labeling requirements and product safety standards. To build consumer trust and uphold the integrity of the handmade soap market, soap makers must approach their art with a dedication to openness, safety, and moral behavior. A conscientious and knowledgeable approach to legal considerations equips soap makers for success in a dynamic and growing industry, as the demand for distinctive and high-quality soap products grows.

Building A Brand and Connecting with Customers

In the handmade soap industry, building a brand and a relationship with customers is a challenging and multifaceted for soap producers. Success in an era where consumers seek for experiences, stories, and authenticity in addition to products depends on building a strong brand identity. This in-depth investigation covers defining brand identity, creating a distinctive brand story, designing efficient packaging, utilizing online and offline marketing strategies, encouraging customer engagement, and adjusting to changing consumer trends. It also covers all the essential components of developing a brand for handmade soaps. In addition to differentiating their goods in a crowded market, soap manufacturers can build enduring relationships with a clientele that appreciates the craftsmanship, high caliber, and unique touch that come with handmade soaps by skillfully navigating these factors.

Understanding brand identification is essential to developing a recognizable handmade soap brand. A soap maker's visual, emotional, and intellectual elements that set their products apart from competitors' are all part of their brand identity. It entails creating a distinctive name, logo, color scheme, and aesthetic that all convey the brand's essence. The visual components should evoke the intended feelings connected to the brand, which should also resonate with the target audience. Building a unified and memorable brand identity lays the groundwork for dependable communication and identification, paving the way for a powerful and identifiable entry into the handmade soap industry.

Creating a distinctive brand story is an essential part of brand identity. A potent technique for developing a stronger connection with consumers is the brand's story. The brand narrative should communicate the enthusiasm, motivation, and principles propelling the soap manufacturer's art. The brand story gives the products a more human touch, whether based on personal experiences, a commitment to sustainability, or a devotion to natural components. Customers may relate to the soap maker's journey and philosophy by connecting with it through various channels, including the brand's website, social media accounts, and packaging. This builds a sense of authenticity and trust.

A successful brand development strategy for handcrafted soaps also includes well-designed packaging. Since the packaging is the product's initial point of contact with the customer, it has great potential to communicate the character and values of the brand. In addition to drawing attention to itself on store shelves or internet platforms, thoughtful and attractive packaging conveys the value and distinctiveness of the product. To create a unified and visually appealing packaging that appeals to the target market, the materials, colors, and design aspects should align with the brand identity. Incorporating sustainable and eco-friendly packaging alternatives also demonstrates a dedication to environmental responsibility and meets the desires of environmentally conscious customers.

A website is essential for customer interaction and brand exposure in the digital age. Creating a polished, easy-to-use website is a central location for displaying handcrafted soaps, telling the brand's narrative, and processing online orders. The website should provide a seamless and safe buying experience while reflecting the business identity through consistent graphic aspects. Customers may easily browse, choose, and buy products thanks to e-commerce features, which helps the brand reach a wider audience outside of local marketplaces. Adopting search engine optimization (SEO) tactics improves the brand's online presence and allows prospective buyers to find the handcrafted soaps via internet searches.

Social media channels are essential for communicating with customers and developing a business. Visual channels like Instagram, Facebook, and Pinterest are available for exhibiting the craftsmanship and distinctiveness of handcrafted soaps. A strong feeling of community and a devoted following are developed through producing engaging and shareable material, such as product images, behind-the-scenes looks, and tutorials. Using social media to communicate their stories, soap producers can engage with consumers directly and share the values, passion, and quality that characterize their brand. Customers can become brand evangelists by interacting with followers via direct messages, comments, and interactive content. This fosters a sense of connection and loyalty.

Offline marketing campaigns also aid in client interaction and brand building in addition to online techniques. One can engage directly with clients by participating in artisanal events, craft fairs, or local markets. Creating an eye-catching booth, providing product samples, and telling the brand's story face-to-face all contribute to memorable encounters that make an impact. Working with neighborhood shops or boutiques for product placement exposes handmade soaps to a larger market and gives the brand more credibility. Connections with other craftspeople or companies for joint ventures or co-branded goods can increase awareness and promote a feeling of community.

Beyond the point of sale, fostering client connection is an ongoing, mutual effort. Customer-centric practices like personalized communication, responsive customer service, and loyalty programs facilitate a successful and long-lasting connection. Promoting client endorsements and reviews offers insightful input and social proof, which affects how prospective buyers regard the company. Quickly responding to customer questions or comments shows consideration and dedication to their needs. Organizing freebies, competitions, or interactive social media campaigns fosters consumer involvement and deepens the relationship between the business and its target market.

One dynamic component of developing a handmade soap brand is adjusting to changing consumer demands. By remaining aware of changes in customer inclinations, environmental standards, and industry advancements, soap manufacturers can modify their approaches and products as necessary. For instance, in response to consumer demand for more sustainable and environmentally friendly products, soap manufacturers may look into other packaging options, use ingredients that have been ethically obtained, or highlight their dedication to moral business practices. Keeping an eye on wellness, aromatherapy, and skincare trends allows soap manufacturers to launch new product lines or formulations catering to customers' interests.

Building customer trust starts with embracing honesty and transparency throughout the brand-building process. Honesty and integrity are promoted through open communication on ingredients, sourcing procedures, and the soap-making process. Sharing behind-the-scenes content or personal experiences that shed light on the struggles and victories of the soap-making process adds a relatable element to the brand. Establishing a strong foundation for enduring customer connections is a continuous process of building trust that calls for consistency in communication and product quality.

Branching out from product sales to include educational content strengthens the soap maker's position as an industry authority. Producing blog articles, guides, or videos about ingredient knowledge, skincare advice, or soapmaking techniques establishes the business as a helpful resource for consumers. In addition to adding value for customers, sharing knowledge highlights the soap maker's skill and love for their work. The brand's reach and influence can be increased by distributing educational content via social media, the website, or partnerships with other content producers.

Finally, developing a brand and engaging with consumers in the handmade soap sector requires a comprehensive strategy that includes customer involvement, packaging design, online and offline marketing, brand identity, narrative, and a dedication to openness. Soap makers need to strike a balance between their love of their craft and business sense if they want to create a brand that appeals to a broad spectrum of discerning consumers. Brands that engage with customers, convey their values authentically, and adjust to shifting consumer tastes stand to benefit from the ongoing evolution of the handmade soap market as well as add to the creativity and vibrancy of the artisanal soap community.

CHAPTER IX

Crafting Clean: Environmental Impact

Analyzing The Ecological Footprint of Commercial Vs. Handmade Soaps

The comparison of handmade and commercial soaps' ecological footprints reveals a multifaceted interaction of elements beyond their ability to clean. Talks about sustainability now center on the soap sector as customers examine the environmental impact of their purchases more closely. Large companies' mass-produced commercial soaps are sometimes criticized for their resource-intensive manufacturing techniques, elaborate packaging, and usage of artificial additives. On the other hand, handmade soaps are manufactured by small-scale producers and artists, and they market themselves as environmentally friendly substitutes by stressing natural ingredients, minor processing, and less waste. This thorough investigation explores the environmental impact of both commercial and handmade soaps, looking into essential areas like where to find raw materials, how soap is created, packaged, transported, and general sustainability measures. By carefully considering these factors, customers may support a more environmentally conscious and sustainable soap industry while making decisions consistent with their values.

The primary component of the ecological footprint of soap manufacture is the source of raw materials. Mass-produced synthetic components generated from petrochemicals in commercial soaps contribute to resource depletion and environmental deterioration.

These synthetic components' extraction, processing, and transportation increases the ecological effect. Handmade soaps, on the other hand, usually emphasize natural and plant-based ingredients that are sourced ethically and sustainably. Because they select botanicals, essential oils, and oils that have been ethically harvested, artisans use fewer extraction techniques that are detrimental to the environment. Handmade soaps' emphasis on ethical raw material sourcing shows a dedication to reducing the environmental impact of the manufacturing process from the beginning.

The environmental effect and resource consumption of the manufacturing procedures used to create handmade vs commercial soaps differ significantly. Large-scale machinery, energy-intensive procedures, and frequently severe chemical reactions are used in commercial soap production. The sheer volume of production results in a considerable amount of trash and pollutants and a massive use of energy and water. In contrast, traditional crafting techniques, manual labor, and smaller-scale machinery are usually used to create handcrafted soap. Handmade soap has a lesser environmental impact due to its more straightforward methods and smaller scale, although energy consumption is still a factor. Because they produce their soap by hand, artisanal soap makers may provide a more personal and intimate relationship with the process, which promotes waste reduction and resource conservation.

Evaluating the environmental impact of soaps, whether handmade or commercial, highlights the significance of packaging. The packaging of commercial soaps is infamous for being extravagant and frequently not recyclable. Bars that are individually wrapped, plastic containers, and complex labeling add up to a substantial environmental impact, especially when you consider the enormous amounts manufactured and consumed worldwide. Producers of handmade soap, aware of the effects of packaging, frequently choose eco-friendly and minimalist strategies. A common choice among artisans is straightforward, recyclable, or biodegradable packaging, demonstrating their dedication to cutting waste and limiting the environmental effect of product display. Handmade soap manufacturers actively address an essential aspect of the ecological footprint by highlighting sustainable packaging techniques, which corresponds with consumer demands for environmentally conscious products.

Another aspect of the ecological footprint is transportation, which includes the movement of completed goods, raw materials, and distribution systems. The production of commercial soap, which is frequently concentrated in sizable manufacturing facilities, necessitates the lengthy transit of raw materials and completed commodities. Major soap companies' international supply networks contribute to air pollution, carbon emissions, and the depletion of scarce resources. On the other hand, handmade soap manufacturers usually run on a smaller scale, procuring locally whenever feasible and reducing emissions associated with transportation. By prioritizing local and regional distribution networks, the carbon footprint from transporting soap ingredients and final product is further mitigated. This localization supports local economies, lessens total environmental effect, and is in line with sustainable principles.

Considerations like product lifetime and end-of-life disposal are included in the lifecycle study of commercial and handmade soaps and the production and transportation phases. Commercial soaps may last longer on the shelf but, when thrown away, can pollute the environment since they frequently contain artificial ingredients and preservatives. The long-term ecological damage is further compounded by the persistence of synthetic chemicals in water systems and the slow breakdown of non-biodegradable packing materials. Though they may have a shorter shelf life, handmade soaps with natural ingredients and little preservatives typically offer a more environmentally benign end of life. Natural soap components' biodegradability and ecologically friendly packaging support the goals of a circular economy by reducing waste and fostering ecological sustainability.

A critical factor in assessing the ecological footprint is the amount of water used in the manufacturing and using soaps. Large-scale manufacturing operations in the commercial soap industry frequently necessitate significant water inputs for processing ingredients, equipment cleaning, and other industrial tasks. The water footprint is further increased when synthetic chemicals are derived from water-intensive crops. Because handmade soap is produced on a smaller scale and emphasizes mindful water consumption, it is typically more water-efficient. Furthermore, homemade soaps are prepared with natural materials rather than synthetic chemicals like commercial soaps, which frequently help minimize water pollution. The water footprint is also influenced by consumer behavior. For example, using handcrafted soaps, which effectively lather with less water, encourages shorter showers and helps conserve water.

Apart from the environmental impact, the ethical and social aspects of soap manufacturing contribute to the industry's overall sustainability. Due to shareholder interests and profit margins, commercial soap manufacture may ignore social responsibility factors like ethical sourcing, fair labor methods, and community involvement. On the other hand, many companies that make handmade soap place a high value on moral issues. They frequently use local communities as their source of ingredients, promote fair trade principles, and maintain open supply chains. Handmade soap production strongly emphasizes community-centric methods, which supports a more socially sustainable business model and satisfies consumer demand for ethically conscious products.

Consumer education and awareness are critical factors in influencing decisions about what to buy that are consistent with environmental ideals. Customers' increased awareness of environmental issues has resulted in a demand boom for eco-friendly and sustainable products like soaps. By supporting makers of handmade soap, who frequently promote ethical sourcing, sustainability, and transparency, customers may make decisions that align with their values. Promoting environmentally friendly practices in the soap sector entails pushing more prominent corporations to act environmentally responsibly and selecting sustainable goods. This change in customer choices and behavior may bring about a more widespread industrial transition toward less ecological impact and increased sustainability.

In conclusion, comparing the environmental impact of homemade vs commercial soaps reveals a complex interaction of variables ranging from the location of raw materials to their disposal at the end of their useful lives. Handmade soaps are more environmentally friendly than professionally manufactured soaps because they focus on natural ingredients, lower production scale, eco-friendly packaging, and local distribution networks. The handmade soap industry aspires to environmental consciousness, transparency, and community engagement whereas the commercial soap industry needs help with resource-intensive methods, elaborate packaging, and worldwide supply chains. With information about the ecological footprint, consumers may significantly influence the development of a sustainable, environmentally conscious, and ethically and ecologically conscious soap sector.

Sustainable Practices in Soap Production

Sustainable methods used in making handmade soap are essential to the expanding trend of ethical and environmentally responsible consumer choices. A movement toward sustainability is occurring in several industries, including soap manufacturing, due to customers' growing demand for products consistent with their beliefs and increasing knowledge of environmental challenges. Producers of handmade soap, who frequently work on a smaller scale, can implement techniques that give priority to ethical sourcing, ecological responsibility, and community involvement. This thorough investigation covers ingredients sourcing, energy use, waste reduction, packaging options, community impact, and the broader ramifications for a soap industry that values environmental stewardship. It also explores the many facets of sustainable practices in the handmade soap production. Handmade soap manufacturers may satisfy a discriminating customer base and further the cause of a more ethical and conscientious approach to soap production by adopting sustainable procedures.

Careful selection of ingredients is the cornerstone of sustainability in the handmade soap industry. The natural and plant-based ingredients used to manufacture artisanal soap frequently precede the synthetic additions and petrochemical-derived substances found in many commercial soaps. The focus on ethical supply chains, fair labor practices, and the environmental impact of ingredient procurement are all part of responsible ingredient sourcing. Sustainable harvesting of oils, butters, and botanicals is a popular choice among artisans, since it guarantees that the cultivation and extraction procedures follow environmentally responsible conservation guidelines. Handmade soap manufacturers provide a product that appeals to consumers looking for sustainable and ethical options by using components with a low environmental impact.

One important consideration when evaluating sustainability is the amount of energy used in the soap-making process. Handmade soap makers can use energy-saving techniques, but commercial soap manufacture frequently uses large-scale technology and energy-intensive procedures. Making soap on a small scale enables a more hands-on approach, wherein traditional manufacturing techniques and human labor lessen the dependence on significant energy use. Some craftspeople also look into alternate energy sources, such solar or wind power, to reduce the environmental effect of their work. This mindful approach to energy use aligns with the overarching objective of lowering the carbon footprint connected to the manufacturing of handcrafted soap.

Waste reduction is a vital component of sustainability in manufacturing handcrafted soap. The vast production and heavy machinery used in the commercial soap industry result in a large amount of waste from byproducts and abandoned materials. On the other hand, artisanal soap producers frequently employ procedures that emphasize producing as little waste as possible. This could involve reusing soap scraps, recycling packaging materials, or developing inventive ways to use leftover ingredients in later batches. Some craftspeople take things a step further and investigate zero-waste soap-making methods to reduce their environmental effect through meticulous resource and waste management across the entire manufacturing process. By implementing waste reduction strategies, handmade soap manufacturers support a more ecologically conscious and sustainable sector.

Sustainable handmade soap production depends heavily on the packaging options chosen. Commercial soaps are well known for their oversized, non-recyclable packaging, which adds to environmental waste and pollution. Producers of handmade soap, aware of how packaging affects the environment, frequently prefer environmentally friendly choices. Many artisans use paper, cardboard, or even biodegradable materials for simple, recyclable packaging. Some companies even go one step further and encourage consumers to adopt a zero-waste mindset by providing solutions without packaging. Handmade soap manufacturers can lessen their environmental impact and satisfy customers looking for eco-friendly options by implementing sustainable packaging techniques.

A key component of sustainable methods in manufacturing handmade soap is the impact on the community. Handcrafted soap producers often interact with nearby communities, attempting to source ingredients locally and endorsing fair trade principles. This focus on the community guarantees that the advantages of soap production go beyond the product itself, improving the lives of people in the supply chain. Through cultivating connections with nearby vendors, craftspeople enhance the financial prosperity of their localities, establishing a support system that conforms to sustainability ideals. Furthermore, some handmade soap makers donate a portion of their earnings to philanthropic causes or community projects, underscoring the social responsibility of producing sustainable soap.

In handmade soap-making, sustainability is primarily supported by ethical and transparent factors. Artisans frequently enlighten customers on their sourcing procedures, ingredients' source, and manufacturing procedures. Thanks to this transparent and honest communication, customers may make educated decisions that are consistent with their beliefs. Fair labor procedures are a component of ethical considerations since they guarantee equitable treatment for all parties involved in the soap-making process. Handmade soap makers not only support a responsible consumer culture by emphasizing transparency and ethical practices but also set an example for the more significant soap business to follow.

Promoting sustainability in making handcrafted soap requires consumer awareness and educational programs. Artists frequently utilize their platforms to inform the public about the advantages of using natural ingredients, the effects of soap production on the environment, and the significance of promoting sustainable methods. Craftspeople enable customers to make decisions consistent with their values by supplying information about the environmental impact of their products. In addition to selling handmade soap, some companies also provide seminars or instructional materials on sustainable living, which inspires customers to embrace green habits outside of soap purchases. This educational effort helps to create a consumer base that is more aware of environmental issues and makes a shared commitment to sustainability.

Eco-labels and certifications offer a formal acknowledgement of sustainable methods used in the making of handcrafted soap. While some craftspeople prioritize obtaining certifications like fair-trade or organic labels, others could place more importance on providing customers with clear and comprehensive information about their methods. A soap maker's certifications can clearly indicate their sustainability efforts and reassure customers who value eco-friendly or ethically conscious products. Though many artisanal soap makers prioritize sustainable practices without pursuing formal certifications, their commitment to ethical and eco-friendly production is communicated through open communication and consumer trust, so the lack of certifications only sometimes indicates a lack of sustainability.

Sustainable practices continue to improve due to cooperation and knowledge exchange within the handmade soap industry. Artists frequently work together, exchanging knowledge, best practices, and creative solutions for producing soap in an environmentally friendly manner. Online discussion boards, workshops, and trade shows allow soap manufacturers to collaborate and discuss sustainability- related issues. As artists learn from one another's experiences and cooperate to improve the overall sustainability of the handmade soap industry, this cooperative method promotes a culture of continual improvement and a sense of community.

To sum up, handmade soap production can be made more sustainably by taking a comprehensive approach that considers the energy and ingredient sourcing, packaging options, waste reduction, community impact, transparency, education, certifications, and cooperative efforts among the artisanal soap community. Handmade soap manufacturers who embrace sustainability meet the growing need for environmentally friendly goods and support a more significant trend of ethical and responsible consumer choices. The sustainable methods used by handcrafted soap manufacturers are crucial in creating an ethical and environmentally conscious soap sector, since consumers prioritize goods that reflect their beliefs.

Educating Consumers on The Benefits of Handmade and Eco-Friendly Soaps

One of the most important ways to cultivate a base of environmentally concerned and conscientious customers is to educate them about the advantages of handcrafted and eco-friendly soaps. Customers are looking for options that support environmental well-being and are consistent with their values as the need for sustainable products rises. Carefully constructed and frequently made with natural materials, handmade soaps are an appealing option for individuals seeking to make environmentally and health-conscious choices. This in-depth investigation explores the many benefits of handmade and environmentally friendly soaps, including transparency about ingredients, environmental effect, benefits for skin health, support for local economies, and broader implications for sustainability in the soap sector. Understanding these advantages enables customers to make well-informed decisions that go beyond personal hygiene practices and positively affect the environment and their well-being.

Ingredient transparency is one of the main advantages of handcrafted and environmentally friendly soaps. Handmade soaps emphasize natural and plant-based components, unlike mass-produced commercial soaps that frequently contain harsh chemicals and synthetic additives. This emphasis increases customers' faith in the product and the soap producer on openness, ensuring they know what they are putting on their skin. Producers of handmade soap frequently provide transparent information about the ingredients they use, including the provenance and characteristics of each ingredient. Not only does this transparency support the tenets of responsible consumerism, but it also allows people to make decisions based on their skincare preferences and needs.

Handmade and environmentally friendly soaps also have a strong positive impact on the environment. Commercial soap manufacturing is typically associated with environmental degradation due to its resource-intensive methods, elaborate packaging, and global supply chains. Handmade soap manufacturers, on the other hand, usually run on a smaller scale and strongly emphasize sustainable methods for obtaining ingredients, using energy, and minimizing waste. Using natural chemicals, ethically sourced botanicals, and environmentally friendly packaging all help lessen their environmental impact. Customers are more likely to prioritize the environment's health when informed about the advantages of handcrafted and eco-friendly soaps for the environment.

Handmade and environmentally friendly soaps have substantial skin health advantages beyond environmental concerns. Commercial soaps can cause irritation or dryness to the skin by depleting it of its natural oils and containing harsh chemicals and synthetic additives. A kinder option that nourishes and hydrates the skin are handmade soaps, which are prepared with natural ingredients and essential oils. Many craftspeople use skin- beneficial oils like coconut, olive, and shea butter, each selected for its unique qualities. Consumers are encouraged to make decisions that support both the environment and their skin's health and well-being when they are informed about these components' nourishing and moisturizing properties.

Choosing handcrafted and eco-friendly soaps has the concrete advantage of promoting local businesses. Artisan soap manufacturers frequently use local suppliers to source their ingredients, enhancing the economic health of their local communities. This focus on regional and local supply chains encourages community involvement and support, which is consistent with the values of ethical and sustainable consumer choices. Educating customers about how their purchases affect regional economies fosters a feeling of accountability and community, highlighting that selecting handcrafted and environmentally friendly soaps benefits the community even outside of personal hygiene.

Handmade and environmentally friendly soaps have an educational value beyond encouraging ethical and sustainable business practices in the soap sector. Numerous craftspeople actively participate in environmental projects, like recycling programs, zero-waste packaging, and energy-efficient manufacturing techniques. Customers who support these methods not only help individual soap producers succeed but also push for a more comprehensive shift in the industry toward sustainability. Customers who are made aware of the combined effects of their decisions are better equipped to advocate for sustainable practices, which can change the course of the soap business as a whole and promote an eco-friendly culture.

Choosing eco-friendly and handcrafted soaps allows customers to match their ideals with their purchases. These soaps are an excellent option for people looking for a holistic and conscientious approach to personal care because they emphasize transparency, environmental responsibility, skin health, and community support. To encourage customers to see their purchasing decisions as a part of a more significant movement towards sustainability and ethical consumerism, the educational process include spreading knowledge about the associated advantages of handmade and environmentally friendly soaps. The demand for handcrafted and environmentally friendly soaps is expected to rise as customers become more knowledgeable and aware of the consequences of their decisions. This will have a beneficial knock-on effect that goes beyond daily routines and helps to create a more sustainable and ethical soap sector.

In conclusion, a critical first step in developing a customer base that is more ecologically conscious and conscientious is educating consumers about the advantages of handcrafted and eco-friendly soaps. The benefits of selecting handmade and environmentally friendly soaps are numerous and significant, ranging from ingredient transparency and environmental effect to skin health benefits and support for local businesses. Soap manufacturers and advocates help to alter consumer behavior toward sustainable and ethical practices by educating consumers about the interrelated advantages of their choices. The increasing need for eco-friendly products means that education plays a crucial role in forming an industry for soap that puts openness, accountability, and a shared commitment to the health of the earth and its inhabitants first.

CHAPTER X

Beyond Soap Making: Crafting a Clean Lifestyle

Extending The Principles of Sustainability to Other Aspects of Life

Taking the ideas of sustainability and applying them to the making of handcrafted soap is a revolutionary path that can change many facets of everyday existence. Even though sustainability has received much attention lately, adopting eco-friendly habits in other areas of life is crucial to building a more peaceful coexistence with the environment. This thorough investigation explores the complex elements of applying sustainability concepts to different facets of life, including food choices, transportation, fashion, household activities, and general consumer behavior. Individuals can help create a more morally and environmentally sensitive lifestyle by adopting sustainability as a guiding principle. This can eventually impact more considerable systemic and societal changes that lead to a more sustainable future.

Sustainable concepts can be easily incorporated into everyday life through household habits, which constitute a fundamental domain. A more sustainable home environment can be achieved by little but effective adjustments including cutting back on trash, conserving water, and using less energy. Reducing the home's carbon footprint can be achieved by installing energy-efficient appliances, using natural lighting, and improving the heating and cooling systems. Rainwater collection, water-saving fixtures, and careful water use all help to conserve resources. The quantity of home garbage in landfills can be decreased by implementing a waste management strategy incorporating recycling, composting, and cutting back on single-use plastics. Individuals who consciously choose to live sustainably not only reduce their impact on the environment, but they also set an example for others in their community.

When it comes to incorporating sustainability concepts into everyday life, transportation decisions are crucial. People are looking for environmentally friendly alternatives to conventional forms of transportation as their knowledge of environmental deterioration and climate change increases. Using public transit, carpooling, biking, or walking cuts carbon emissions, eases traffic congestion, and lessens dependency on fossil fuels. For people needing personal mobility, switching to electric or hybrid automobiles is more environmentally friendly. Further reducing the need for daily transportation is the trend towards remote work and virtual meetings, which technological improvements have driven. This presents an opportunity to incorporate sustainability into professional life. People can lessen the environmental effect of regular travel by reevaluating their options for transportation and looking into eco-friendly options.

A significant area of daily living where sustainability concepts can be strongly ingrained is in food choices. The global food system has a significant environmental impact on everything from farming practices to food transportation. Making deliberate decisions that prioritize local, seasonal, and organic products is a crucial component of implementing sustainable eating habits. Lowering meat intake or switching to plant-based diets aligns with sustainable practices because raising animals contributes significantly to deforestation and greenhouse gas emissions. By encouraging a direct relationship between customers and their food source, such as through community-supported agriculture (CSA), local farmers' markets, or food cooperatives, one can lessen the environmental impact of long-distance food transportation. People can help create a food system that is both socially and environmentally responsible by incorporating sustainability into their food choices.

Another area where the concepts of sustainability can have a significant impact on day-to-day decisions is fashion and garment use. The environmental consequences of the fast fashion business, which are marked by overconsumption, excessive waste, and exploitative labor practices, have spurred a growing movement towards sustainable and ethical fashion. Selecting classic, well-made items, adopting retro or secondhand apparel, and promoting eco-friendly fashion labels all help to lessen the fashion industry's environmental effect. "Less is more" consumption is encouraged and the disposable aspect of quick fashion is discouraged. Daily fashion decisions are further aligned with sustainability ideals by choosing natural and eco-friendly fabrics, taking proper care of one's clothing, and learning about clothing manufacturers' sourcing and production processes. Individuals can actively contribute to the transition towards a more sustainable and ethical fashion scene by critically analyzing and altering their clothes consumption habits.

Consumer behavior increasingly integrates sustainability into general lifestyle decisions rather than specific categories. Choosing products with small ecological footprints, supporting businesses that promote sustainability, and thinking about the social and environmental effects of purchases are all parts of mindful purchasing. Selecting reusable and repairable products over throwaway or single-use ones encourages a culture of longevity and lowers waste production overall. Making thoughtful decisions about electronics, household appliances, and other products can result in lower energy usage and a more conscientious use of resources. People have power over markets when they support sustainability in their purchase decisions, pushing companies to prioritize ethical and environmentally friendly operations.

One crucial area where sustainability ideas can be incorporated into daily living is energy use in the home. Switching to renewable energy sources, such wind or solar power, lowers carbon emissions related to electricity production and lessens dependency on fossil fuels. Adopting intelligent energy management systems, insulating homes, and employing energy-efficient appliances are a few examples of energy-efficient measures that may be implemented to help save energy overall. Further reducing daily energy consumption are lifestyle modifications including disconnecting electronics, turning off lights when not in use, and using energy-efficient water heating techniques. People can lessen their ecological footprint and help the larger society shift to sustainable and renewable energy sources by developing an awareness of how they use energy.

Water conservation techniques used in the house support the proper use of this limited resource and are consistent with sustainability concepts. Water use in homes can be considerably decreased by taking easy steps like quickly patching leaks, installing water-efficient fixtures, and using appliances that maximize water use. Water conservation can be achieved by implementing water-conscious behaviors including turning off faucets when not in use, taking shorter showers, and only running full loads through washing machines and dishwashers. To further enhance water conservation within the home, rainwater harvesting devices can be used for non-potable needs such as garden watering. Individuals can mitigate the demand on water supplies and actively contribute to sustainable water management by incorporating water saving methods into their everyday activities.

Creating outside environments with green spaces and home gardening offers a chance to apply sustainability concepts. Using organic gardening techniques, embracing permaculture concepts, and cultivating native plants increase biodiversity, lessen the need for chemical inputs, and build resilient ecosystems. Outdoor activities can align with sustainable principles by implementing rainwater harvesting for garden irrigation, composting kitchen waste for nutrient-rich soil, and performing integrated pest management. Green places that neighbors, such as community gardens share, provide a platform for group sustainable initiatives that promote environmental care. Adopting sustainable gardening techniques allows people to improve not just their immediate environment but also the more enormous ecological well-being of their communities.

Reducing trash and managing garbage responsibly are essential elements of sustainability that may be easily incorporated into everyday life. Repurposing materials, reducing the number of single-use items, and sorting waste for recycling are all part of adopting the reduce, reuse, and recycle philosophy. Completing the circle in the natural decomposition cycle, composting organic kitchen waste helps create nutrient-rich soil for gardening. Responsible waste management can be achieved by participating in neighborhood recycling programs, paying attention to product packaging, selecting products made of recyclable materials, and choosing minimal or eco-friendly packaging. People actively help to lessen the total environmental impact connected with garbage disposal by choosing wisely when it comes to consumption and waste generation.

Promoting a culture of sustainability that goes beyond personal decisions requires education and awareness. People enable themselves to make meaningful decisions by learning about environmental challenges, appreciating the effects of their daily actions, and never ceasing to learn about sustainable practices. Community, business, and school-based educational efforts serve as additional means of disseminating sustainability principles and fostering a shared knowledge of the interdependence of individual activities and more significant environmental concerns. Living sustainably is not just a personal decision; it is also a social obligation that calls for constant learning, discussion, and lobbying for structural adjustments that consider ethical and environmental concerns.

Applying sustainability principles to diverse facets of life necessitates a deliberate and comprehensive approach to everyday decisions and actions. People can actively contribute to a more environmentally conscious and morally aligned lifestyle by incorporating sustainability into their home practices, transportation, food choices, fashion, consumer behavior, energy consumption, water usage, outdoor activities, waste reduction, and educational initiatives. In addition to impacting people's well-being, this movement towards sustainability also helps bring about the more significant social change required to solve urgent environmental issues. In the end, adopting a sustainable lifestyle in many spheres of life signifies a dedication to conscientious living and developing a more peaceful coexistence with the environment.

Encouraging A Mindful and Clean Approach to Daily Living

To promote a clean and thoughtful way of life, one must make a comprehensive commitment to making intelligent decisions that prioritize one's health, the sustainability of the environment, and a positive relationship with one's surroundings. This way of thinking transcends individual behavior and penetrates many facets of daily existence to foster a feeling of cleanliness and alertness that appeals to individuals and society.

Being in the present and deliberately choosing decisions that support one's ideals and general well-being are the cornerstones of a mindful way of life. When mindfulness is applied to one's behaviors, it shows itself as an awareness of one's body, thoughts, and emotions while engaging in daily tasks. People can incorporate mindfulness into their daily activities, from the straightforward act of washing their hands to the more involved chores of cooking or working, to develop a stronger sense of present-moment awareness and a better appreciation for the inherent beauty in everyday tasks.

Maintaining personal hygiene and practicing environmental stewardship are essential elements of a mindful way of life. Personal hygiene helps maintain physical health and well-being by halting the transmission of disease and encouraging self-care. Keeping one's living area tidy and orderly goes hand in hand with personal hygiene, fostering an atmosphere that promotes peace of mind and calm. Clean living spaces align with the mindful living tenets of stress reduction, improved attention, and relaxation haven.

The principles of mindful and clean living also apply to eating choices, emphasizing wholesome, whole foods that support mental and physical health. A food plan rich in vegetables, fruits, and whole grains not only enhances health but also shows environmental consciousness through dietary choices. Savoring every bite, paying attention to signals of hunger and fullness, and enjoying the food's journey from farm to plate are all components of mindful eating.

Reducing meat consumption, promoting local and sustainable agriculture, and avoiding food waste are mindful dietary decisions that lead to a more sustainable and clean food system.

One of the most important ways to promote a clean, thoughtful way of living is by environmental consciousness. Making deliberate decisions regarding the things we use and their effects on the environment is a crucial component of mindful consumption. Choosing sustainable and environmentally friendly products, cutting out on single-use items, and managing trash responsibly all fit into the aware and clean-living concepts. Making decisions that put environmental sustainability first and considering the entire life cycle of products—from manufacturing to disposal—are essential to reducing one's ecological footprint.

Engaging in interpersonal connections and community service are additional benefits of practicing mindfulness. To engage in mindful conversation, one must practice active listening, empathy, and genuine presence. Clear and constructive communication lowers conflict, promotes healthy relationships, and helps create a pleasant and encouraging social atmosphere. Completing deeds of kindness, volunteering, and taking part in community projects demonstrate a dedication to the welfare of the larger community as well as oneself, emulating the values of cleanliness and mindfulness in a group setting.

Cultivating activities that support emotional resilience and stress reduction is part of a mindful and clean approach to mental health. Deep breathing techniques, yoga, and mindfulness meditation help dynamic equilibrium, mental clarity, and increased self-awareness. Including these activities in daily life promotes mental well-being and strengthens the link between the mind and body. People prioritizing their mental health provide the groundwork for a more conscientious and structured way of living.

Promoting a clean and thoughtful way of living is accomplished mainly through educational programs. Giving people knowledge about the advantages of sustainable living, mindfulness, and clean living options enables them to make wise decisions. Education initiatives in businesses, communities, and schools can increase understanding of how individual choices affect the environment and society more broadly. By promoting an environment that values ongoing education and information exchange, society can adopt a more conscientious and hygienic way of living.

In summary, promoting a clean and thoughtful way of living requires making deliberate decisions that put the health of the individual, the sustainability of the environment, and constructive community involvement first. Routine activities are infused with mindfulness, which promotes a closer relationship with the present and an awareness of the beauty in everyday actions. Orderliness, mental clarity, and physical health are all enhanced by cleanliness, both in one's surroundings and in one's routines. People contribute to a more thoughtful and clean way of living that resonates on a personal and societal level by extending these principles to nutritional choices, interpersonal relationships, mental well-being, and community engagement. Society can adopt these ideals and cultivate a culture that values making conscious decisions and embodies a harmonious relationship with oneself, others, and the environment by raising awareness and educating people.

Inspiring Readers to Take Action in Creating a Cleaner, Greener World

Urging people to become involved in designing a sustainable future by taking action and making the world a cleaner, greener place is a call to action that goes beyond written words. Literature has the unmatched capacity to arouse empathy and spark the imagination, which makes it a powerful force for change. Through gripping stories, educational texts, and thought-provoking works, literature has the power to inspire readers to take meaningful action, ignite a sense of duty, and raise environmental consciousness.

A literary bridge connecting readers to the pressing problems facing our world is provided by environmental literature, which includes genres including eco-fiction, nature writing, and environmental non-fiction. These literary works create a sense of connection between readers and the environment by displaying the profound effects of human activity and engrossing them in the beauty of the natural world. Writing can arouse in readers a deep sense of responsibility and drive them to contemplate their place in the larger ecological narrative, whether through the vivid descriptions of immaculate landscapes or the severe portrayal of environmental destruction.

Finding inspiration frequently comes from realizing how individual decisions have an impact on the entire world. In addition to teaching readers about the complex web of ecosystems, environmental literature emphasizes how particular choices have a cascading influence on the environment. Reading about the effects of pollution, deforestation, climate change, and biodiversity loss encourages readers to consider their own lives and the possible ramifications of their daily choices. Readers are inspired to embrace sustainable habits and promote environmental stewardship by this newly discovered knowledge, which catalyzes change.

Literary works have an extraordinary power to arouse empathy and emotional resonance beyond simple information transmission. Literature humanizes the environmental story by drawing readers into the hardships of characters facing environmental issues or highlighting the accomplishments of those committed to conservation. As a result of this emotional connection, readers are driven to take action out of a genuine concern for the welfare of the world and its inhabitants, in addition to a sense of obligation.

Fostering a shared environmental consciousness can be facilitated by literature, as environmental advocacy frequently depends on a collective grasp of the issues involved. Readers can participate in meaningful discussions about sustainability, climate change, and conservation through book clubs, discussion forums, and educational initiatives around environmental literature. These group talks provide forums for knowledge sharing, idea sharing, and cooperative efforts to make the planet greener and cleaner. In this situation, literature acts as a catalyst to create groups of environmentally conscious people motivated to take coordinated action.

The potential for literature to inspire concrete action is just as potent as its capacity to elicit strong feelings and transmit information. Calls to action are a common feature of environmental literature, offering readers doable actions they may take to have a positive impact. Whether pushing for governmental changes, encouraging eco-friendly activities, or lowering carbon footprints, literature is a roadmap for converting ideas into practical actions. Literature turns indifference into action by providing readers with a road map, enabling them to participate in the group effort to make the world greener and cleaner.

In conclusion, literature effectively and gracefully aims to motivate readers to take action toward a cleaner, greener future. Literature is a beacon directing readers toward significant change by vividly illustrating environmental challenges, encouraging emotional connection, creating a shared ecological consciousness, and offering helpful summons to action. Readers become aware of their capacity to be stewards of a sustainable and thriving planet as they interact with the stories, characters, and insights found in environmental literature. This leads readers on a journey of individual and societal transformation.

CONCLUSION

Conclusively, "Crafting Clean: The Art and Science of Handmade Soap" captures the complex process of converting basic materials into a sensory and moral encounter. During this investigation, we have explored the fine line between creativity and science, revealing the painstaking workmanship that goes into making handmade soaps. The artisan's skill and the fundamental knowledge of the chemical reactions between fats, oils, and lye highlight that manufacturing soap is an artistic endeavor in and of itself rather than just a practical one.

Conscious ingredient selection, which promotes regional and fair-trade producers, is a recurring motif. This approach goes beyond simple manufacturing considerations; it is a dedication to ethical sourcing, promoting social responsibility and community involvement. The progression through soap-making methods, such as Melt and Pour, Hot Process, and Cold Process, highlights the wide range of artistic options accessible to craftspeople. Every method showcases the artistry of the craftsman and enables one-of-a-kind soap-making emotions.

In addition to serving as mediums for creative expression, colors, scents, and additives become crucial elements in establishing the soap brand. By carefully combining these components, soap is transformed from a simple cleaning agent into a customised, opulent ritual. The examination of patterns and design digs into the craftsmanship involved, showing how the process of manufacturing soap becomes a medium for artistic expression, with swirls and marbles emerging as distinguishing elements of these handmade masterpieces.

The move towards organic and natural soap varieties reflects a broader consumer trend toward clean and sustainable living. Because handcrafted soaps are manufactured with eco-friendly components, so they are both a stylish and moral decision, in line with current environmental concerns. Considering formulas for sensitive skin and those free of allergens highlights inclusion, acknowledging the range of consumer needs, and adopting a customer-centric mindset.

Herbal and aromatherapy infusions give soapmaking a more holistic touch, nourishing mental and emotional health in addition to the physical act of cleaning. The way that technology and nature combine to make soap highlights how much more than simply a product it can be; it can be a way to take care of oneself and find some peace amid the everyday grind. The artisan's dedication to reducing the environmental effect of the whole soap-making process is further cemented by using environmentally friendly and sustainable packaging options.

It becomes clear that supporting regional and fair-trade suppliers is a behavior based on civic involvement and moral business conduct. The investigation explores the social and economic aspects of soap making while diving into the nuances of ethical ingredient sourcing. In addition to improving community well-being, artists cultivate a sense of moral responsibility within their craft by prioritizing fair-trade and locally produced goods.

As the process of creating soap progresses, minimizing the environmental impact of the sourcing process becomes crucial. The study investigates how decisions about packaging, shipping, and ingredient selection affect the total ecological footprint of soap manufacture. Artisans working together result in greener and cleaner procurement techniques.

As this journey ends, it is clear that creating handcrafted soap is more than simply a craft; it is a way of life that incorporates moral decisions, environmental stewardship, and a dedication to excellence. Every aspect, from the chemistry of creating soap to the creative expression in design, is a brushstroke on the bigger picture of a movement towards sustainable, conscious living. One bar of soap at a time, the soap maker is not only a producer; they are also an artist, a defender of tradition, and an advocate for a greener, cleaner world.

Thank you for buying and reading/ listening to our book. If you found this book useful/ helpful please take a few minutes and leave a review on the platform where you purchased our book. Your feedback matters greatly to us.

9 798869 273758